WHAT IS CHRISTIANITY ?

WHAT IS CHRISTIANITY?

By ADOLF HARNACK

Translated into English by
THOMAS BAILEY SAUNDERS

With an Introduction by
The Very Rev. W. R. MATTHEWS
DEAN OF ST. PAUL'S

FIFTH EDITION

LONDON
ERNEST BENN LIMITED

First Published by
Williams and Norgate Limited

Fifth Edition 1958
Published by Ernest Benn Limited
Bouverie House · Fleet Street · London · EC4

Printed in Great Britain

AUTHOR'S PREFACE TO THE ENGLISH EDITION

To meet the wishes of my English friends I have assented to the publication of these Lectures in English as well as in German, and as my esteemed friend Mr. Bailey Saunders was so self-denying and obliging as to undertake the translation of them, I was sure of their being in the best hands. Whether there is as great a need in England as there is in Germany for a short and plain statement of the Gospel and its history I do not know. But this I know : the theologians of every country only half discharge their duties if they think it enough to treat of the Gospel in the recondite language of learning and bury it in scholarly folios.

BERLIN   A. HARNACK

TRANSLATOR'S PREFACE TO THE FIRST EDITION

The following Lectures were delivered extempore to a class of some six hundred students drawn from all the Faculties in the University of Berlin. An enthusiastic listener took them down in shorthand, and at the close surprised Professor Harnack with a complete report of what he had said. A few alterations sufficed to transform the Lectures into a Book, and German readers everywhere were thus happily enabled to share in some of the privileges of the original audience.

I deem it an honour to have any hand in offering to my fellow-countrymen a similar advantage. Goethe, writing in his last years to Carlyle, described translators, in grandiloquent language, as the agents of intellectual commerce among the nations. The duties of such agency in regard to the contents of this volume I have done my best to discharge, convinced as I am that in the traffic in ideas between Germany and the English-speaking peoples all over the world both the matter of Professor Harnack's discourse and the spirit in which he treats it are alike worthy of attention.

TO THE THIRD EDITION

As a third edition of this work is required I have revised the translation, and I hope that I may have rendered it clearer than it was previously. For some of the improvements I am indebted to friends.

That these Lectures have been worth the attention of the English-speaking peoples is shown by the admiration which they have everywhere won from good judges of their learning, their eloquence, and their sincerity. But, as was to be expected, they have also provoked much dissent. The objections raised to them in England do not seem, to me at least, equal in force or in interest to those raised elsewhere, but, whatever their value, I have endeavoured to meet them in a little book called *Professor Harnack and his Oxford Critics*.

"After a period of specialisation," writes Professor Harnack in his preface to a new edition of the original, "we are about to enter upon a synthetic age, in which it is easier for religion to obtain a hearing. May these Lectures be destined to help in making the new synthesis clear and profound, an emancipating and a civilising influence."

LONDON   T. BAILEY SAUNDERS

CONTENTS

INTRODUCTION

By The Very Rev. W. R. MATTHEWS

LECTURE ONE

Many despair of knowing the truth about Jesus but the truth must still be sought because the past still influences the present. This enquiry will be historical, using the gospel records and the history of the church as sources. It will enable us to extract what is of permanent value from what is merely transitory

LECTURE TWO

The sources of our knowledge of Jesus are the first three gospels. They are from the earliest Jewish Christian circles. The miracles they record do not detract from their historical value which lies in their account of Jesus' teaching, his vocation, and the impression he made on his disciples

LECTURE THREE

John the Baptist taught that a man was pleasing to God through repentance and righteous living. Jesus accepted this and also reinterpreted the accepted Jewish doctrine of God. The coming of the kingdom meant the reign of God in the hearts of individual men

LECTURE FOUR

The kingdom of God is seen in the activity of Jesus. He called individuals to him, healed their sickness and forgave their sin. He taught that God is the Father of all men and each human soul has infinite value. A man's love of God is to be measured by his love of his neighbour

CONTENTS

LECTURE SIXTEEN

INTRODUCTION

THE BOOK here presented to the reader is Bailey Saunders'
lively translation of Adolf Harnack's *Das Wesen des Christentums*, which embodied lectures given to students in the University of Berlin in the winter of 1899–1900 and was published in
German in the latter year. The English version appeared in
1901. The lectures were addressed to hearers who had no theological learning but were concerned to know where Christianity
stood in view of historical criticism. They differ from another
famous series of lectures given in the same university—Schleiermacher's Addresses to the Cultured Despisers of Religion—in
that, though in a sense "apologetic," they assume a readiness to
hear and some understanding of the nature of religious experience. The book caused a considerable stir when it was published
and, as we shall see, exerted an influence which endured beyond
the occasion of its first appearance.

The reputation of the author secured for it a large audience
from the first. Adolf Harnack was at the height of his powers
when he produced the one "popular" work in the long array
of his publications and was recognised as one of the leading
scholars in the field of the history of the early Church. Probably
it would be true to say that he was the greatest living authority
on the literature of the first three Christian centuries and his
mastery of the material had recently been demonstrated in his
massive *History of Dogma*, the final volume of which appeared
in the year in which he began these lectures on the essence of
Christianity. No one doubted, and no one doubts now, that they
are the product of the mind of a great scholar.

Adolf Harnack was born in 1851, the son of a Professor of
Theology. From the first he was subjected to the influence of two
great traditions—Lutheran piety and the ethos of German professorial learning. His career was wholly occupied by university

I

work. He held professorial chairs in Giessen, Marburg and Berlin. As we may see from his lectures, however, he was not of the type of German professor who, absorbed in research, has little knowledge of, or interest in, what goes on in the world or the Church beyond the walls of the university. Harnack did not forget that the study of theology has to do with religion as it is lived by the common man, nor did he fall into the error of supposing that the Kingdom of God had nothing to do with social problems. A more specific influence on his thought must be mentioned. He had a considerable affinity with the theology of Ritschl, who played an important part in the religious thought of Germany in the latter part of the 19th century. Ritschl had two fundamental convictions : first, that religion must be rescued from dependence on metaphysics and philosophy and, secondly, that the historical Jesus whom we encounter in the Gospels is the centre of Christian faith, and that our relation with him determines our spiritual condition. Ritschl was sceptical about the competence of reason to determine the nature of reality and held that we find God through Jesus and not through the dialectics of the intellect. For him the moral consciousness is the organ of religious knowledge. Associated with this point of view was a distrust of mysticism and of the philosophies, such as Platonism, which are allied with it. "The Absolute," he declared, "is an idol."

In Harnack's *History of Dogma* the Ritschlian distrust of philosophy is manifest. Though he admits that the intrusion of Greek philosophy into the thought of the Church was an historical necessity, he holds that the development of dogma, in which ideas and categories of Platonism played a decisive part, involved a departure from the simplicity and freedom of the Gospel. As we may read in these lectures, he conceived that the task and mission of Protestantism was to lead to a new spiritual freedom from dogma and thus to complete the work which Luther began. The other dominant theme of Ritschlian theology, the historical Jesus, is plainly the inspiration of the present book. It tries to answer the questions, What may we know of Jesus as he was, and What does he mean to us?

Harnack died in 1930, having lived long enough to see the

reaction against the Liberal Protestantism of which he had been the most powerful exponent, but before then he had enriched the history of early Christianity with several notable contributions, among which we will refer to the *History of Ancient Christian Literature up to Eusebius* and *The Mission and Expansion of Christianity in the First Three Centuries*, the final edition of which appeared in 1924.

Impersonal and objective in tone as most of his writings are, no one can read them without forming an idea of the writer. His spirit shines through them, the spirit of one whose immense learning is the outcome of a life dedicated to scholarship, of one who sincerely seeks to know the truth and to whom religion is the most momentous of realities, and whether we agree with his conclusions or not, we cannot doubt that he loved and reverenced the Lord Jesus.

It is not the function of an Introduction to save the reader the trouble of reading the book, but to draw attention to some points of interest and to indicate its place in the history of thought. All summaries of a work of real importance must be to some extent misleading, and this is pre-eminently true when, as in *What is Christianity?*, the writer is expressing deep personal convictions. Harnack's view of the essence of Christianity has been summed up by saying that he reduces it to two beliefs: the Fatherhood of God and the Brotherhood of Man. This is not precisely a misinterpretation of Harnack, because these two convictions do, in fact, comprise the dogmatic content of his version of the Christian faith, but it is a misrepresentation, because the bald statement gives no indication of the wealth of meaning and emotion that Harnack finds in the two fundamental affirmations. He himself says that the teaching of Jesus may be grouped under three heads, each of which is of such a nature as to contain the whole. The heads are, "The Kingdom of God and its coming; God the Father and the infinite value of the human soul; the higher righteousness and the commandment of love." He means that, by considering any one of these three heads in all its implications, we may grasp the whole message of Jesus. Harnack is persuaded that the religion of Jesus is both simple and profound. "That Jesus' message is so great and so powerful lies in the fact that it is so simple and, on the other hand, so rich; so simple as to be exhausted in each of the leading thoughts that he uttered; so rich that every one of these thoughts seems to be inexhaustible and the full meaning of the sayings and parables beyond our reach. But more than that—he himself stands behind everything that he said. His words speak to us across the centuries with the freshness of the present. It is here that that profound saying is truly verified : 'Speak that I may see thee.' " Here we have the heart of Harnack's conception of the essence of Christianity : it is the religion of Jesus and capable of being grasped and lived by the ignorant and simple as well as by the learned; it does not depend on theology or philosophy; it springs from the mind and heart of Jesus and his intuitive knowledge of God, and it is kindled in the hearts of others who hear his words in the Gospels: "cor ad cor loquitur."

A notable feature of Harnack's lectures is his confidence that he can rely on the Gospels for an accurate account of the teaching and personality of Jesus. Germany had been the home of the "higher criticism" of the Gospels and much of this had been destructive. Harnack, himself, some years later took part in a controversy on the question whether Jesus had ever existed as an historical individual. To him, however, such radical scepticism seemed absurd. Though he agreed that there were no sufficient materials for the writing of a biography of Jesus, rejecting not only the early chapters of Luke and Matthew but the greater part of the Gospel of John as worthless from the point of view of historical evidence, he appears to have no doubt that the first three Gospels furnish an authentic and sufficient picture of the Teacher and the Man. "They offer us a plain picture of Jesus' teaching, in regard both to its main features and to its individual application; they tell us how his life issued in the service of his vocation; they describe to us the impression which he made upon his disciples, and which they transmitted."

Obviously, the attempt to elicit from the Gospels the abiding core of the teaching of Jesus and to distinguish it from the temporary elements which were due to the religious and intellectual conditions of period and place is, at least in some degree, "subjective" and must be guided to some extent by the value judgments of the historian, but Harnack evidently believed that all men of any spiritual perception would reach the same conclusion. On this point his construction of the original Gospel has been most severely criticised and he has been accused of finding in Jesus the ideal liberal. Harnack, himself, was aware of the danger, for he writes: "It is somewhat touching to observe how anxious everyone is to rediscover himself, together with his own point of view and his own circle of interest, in this Jesus Christ; or at least to get a share in him." Perhaps Harnack would have given greater prominence to the Apocalyptic background of many of Jesus' utterances, if he had not been a 19th-century liberal.

And this observation brings us to the treatment of the Kingdom of God in these lectures. Harnack, as we have seen, rightly put the Kingdom at the centre of Jesus' teaching. He recognises, of course, that in many passages the Kingdom is spoken of as in the future, as a rule of God to be established at the end of the present age. But this conception is not easily assimilable by a liberal philosophy of progress or by the individualist type of spiritual experience. To Harnack, then, all this imagery of the great consummation, of the coming of the Son of Man in the clouds of heaven and of the Judgment, belongs to the temporary and inessential material in the Gospels; it is the protective "bark," or the husk, of the real grain. The Kingdom of God as a present possession, among us or within us, is the unchanging truth in Christ's teaching. The Kingdom of God is the rule of God in the hearts of men; it is identical with eternal life.

Dogma is, then, not the essence of Christianity. But it would be an excessive simplification to allege that Harnack dismisses all doctrines as of no validity. He recognises that some of them at least are formulations of religious experience. The central dogma of traditional Christianity is the Incarnation and the divinity of Christ, and any statement of the nature of the Christian faith which simply denied or ignored this doctrine would at once separate itself from the main stream of Christian thought and experience. It is not easy to determine where Harnack stands in this matter. As we should expect, he does not regard the orthodox formulas of the Council of Chalcedon as relevant to the knowledge of God, which is the one thing needful. They are examples of the intellectualising of the Gospel through the employment of categories of Greek thought. But he has no doubt that Jesus thought of himself as the Son of God in a unique sense and that the Apostolic Church, when it proclaimed its creed, "Jesus is Lord," was expressing not only its belief in the Resurrection, but the impression which this unique consciousness of Sonship had made upon the original disciples. Harnack accepts as authentic the words in Matthew, "No man knoweth the Son but the Father; neither knoweth any man the Father, save the Son, and he to whomsoever the Son will reveal him." Commenting on this passage, Harnack remarks, "Jesus is convinced that he knows God in a way in which no one ever knew him before, and he knows that it is his vocation to communicate this knowledge of God to others by word and by deed —and with it the knowledge that men are God's children." Thus it was, Harnack adds, that he knew himself to be called to be *the* Son of God and could speak of "*my* God and *my* Father" with a meaning which "belongs to no one but himself."

We must own that we are left, after reading the eloquent passages in which Harnack deals with Christology, still in some perplexity; we have no clear answer to the question, Does Harnack believe that Christ was divine in the sense that the Church was right in offering him not only loyalty, but worship? In pursuing this question further, it is well to remember that Schleiermacher, who, like Harnack, deplored the importation of metaphysics into theology, based his doctrine of the Person of Christ on the perfect "God-consciousness" of the Saviour, which is another way of saying "knowledge of God"—and there is no doubt that Schleiermacher intended to justify the worship of Christ by the Church.

We may pass over the other great doctrine—the Atonement —more briefly, with the observation that Harnack has little to say about it. A criticism of his interpretation of the Gospels is that he subordinates the acts of the Lord to his teaching. The writers of the Gospels evidently believed that the death of Jesus

was the most significant fact that they had to relate. The proportion of space devoted to the Passion in all four Gospels
would alone be sufficient evidence of their conviction, but when
we turn to the earliest Gospel, St. Mark, the case becomes even
clearer. That Gospel is primarily the account of something done
—something which culminated, and was completed, in the Cross
and Resurrection. A view which suggests that the crucifixion
was almost an accidental consequence of the Lord's teaching, or
that there would have been a Christian Gospel had there been
no cross, can hardly be said to represent the point of view of the
records, nor that of Jesus himself, as we gather it from
them.

No doubt this criticism of Harnack's lectures was prominent
in the minds of the contemporary critics who repudiated his
"reduced Christianity"; it will be prominent in the minds of
many who read them to-day. In justice to Harnack, we must
remember that, if the tragic sense of life seems to be lacking
in his conception of the Gospel, he wrote at the end of the 19th
century when the tragic was less obtrusive than it is to-day. No
doubt, he shared the feeling of optimism which then prevailed
and supposed that, in spite of setbacks and vicissitudes, the way
was open for peaceful progress. We, who have lived through
two world wars and their aftermath, have a different outlook.
We have good reason to know the power of evil and the temptation to despair. Sunny confidence in the gradual diffusion of
the knowledge of God appears to us insufficient in a world which
trembles on the edge of catastrophe. We may understand better
than those who lived before the break-up of civilisation began
why Paul put his faith in a divine Redeemer who suffered in
and for the darkened world.

Harnack seems often to write as though he considered the
Church to be a necessary evil. This is, of course, an exaggera-
tion, for he certainly held that the fellowship of believers was a
necessary consequence of the proclamation of the Gospel, but
organisation, beyond what is strictly essential to the existence of
the fellowship, to him appeared dangerous to the freedom of the
spiritual life. As a historian, he saw that the episcopal government which developed in the early Church, and the growth of

creed and discipline, were means by which the Gospel was preserved from being lost in the flux of events and opinions, or
overwhelmed by persecution, but he regarded institutions, on the
whole, as, at the best, protective "bark" and, at the worst, as a
heavy weight on the freedom of the spirit. In his chapters on
"Catholicism" and "Greek Catholicism" he applies the touchstone of the "simple" Gospel with devastating effect—the more
devastating because of his charitable readiness to recognise the
signs that the Gospel is still to be heard in those Churches
even amid what he regards as superstition and ecclesiastical
tyranny.

It need not be said that his view of the Church was hotly
contested then as it is now, and not without reason; for the
idea of the Church is more prominent in the New Testament
than Harnack seems to allow and it would be hard to justify
the distinction between Gospel and Church from the writings of
St. Paul. An important result of the publication of *What is
Christianity?* was the beginning of the Modernist movement in
the Roman Catholic Church. This happened, not as a result of
agreement by Roman Catholic scholars with Harnack's views,
but as a reaction against them.

In 1902 the Abbé Alfred Loisy published his short book
L'Evangèle et l'Eglise, which was a reply to Harnack's *Das
Wesen des Christentums* and an attack upon the whole Liberal
Protestant position. This would not have attracted any special
attention, but for the arresting fact that Loisy wrote from a
standpoint which was more "advanced" in its criticism of the
New Testament than Harnack's; for example, he rejects as
probably not an authentic saying of Jesus the text (Matt. 11,
2–7) on which Harnack had based his interpretation of the
divine Sonship of Jesus. The burden of Loisy's book is that
Harnack's whole purpose is misconceived, because it is impossible to separate the Jesus of history from the tradition of the
Church. The meaning of Christianity is to be found by a study
of the history of the Church, and apart from that we can know
nothing of Jesus. He is known to us only through the tradition
of the primitive Church, and what he means to the world is to
be discerned in what his Church has experienced and defined.

The final sentence of Loisy's book sums up the argument: "This little book is full enough if it has shown how Christianity has lived in the Church and by the Church, and how futile is the desire to save it by a search after its quintessence."

As we know, the career of Modernism in the Roman Catholic Church was short and, after his excommunication, Loisy moved away from the Christian faith, though he never ceased to hold that his refutation of Harnack was valid. Probably he had little influence on Protestant theology, and if the *Wesen des Christentums* is now widely thought to be "dated" we must look elsewhere for the reasons.

The study of the New Testament has moved on. The view held by Harnack and the "liberal" school of his time on the sources of the Gospels has been modified by the theory of "Form Criticism," which proposes to get behind the written sources—Mark and the supposed "Q"—and to discover the units of narrative and teaching out of which the Gospels have largely been built up. There is the further aim of forming some idea of how these units came into existence—how, that is, they found a place in the "tradition." The consequences of the application of this method of inquiry are not yet clear and there is much controversy on details. More than one opinion is possible about the value of the results so far achieved, but there is no doubt that Form Criticism has come to stay, and even if it can explain much less than is claimed, it reinforces the contention that the tradition in the Church is a primary source of our knowledge of Jesus, if not the only source. Of course, Form Criticism cannot refute Harnack's presentation of the message of Jesus, but so far as it goes it seems to lend some support to Loisy's objections.

Of greater importance is the new attention given to the eschatology of the Gospels and the importance in them of Apocalyptic ideas. Albert Schweitzer's book *The Quest of the Historical Jesus* had a profound effect in discrediting the Liberal Protestant picture of Jesus and his Gospel. There is no need to recapitulate the theses of this well-known work. Its interest for us in this introduction to Harnack's lectures is that Schweitzer flatly denies the whole basis of Harnack's construction.

Schweitzer's long account of attempts to write a life of Jesus is intended to show that all have failed, and they have failed chiefly because the authors were, consciously or unconsciously, seeking a person after their own image, perhaps, as in the case of Harnack, a man of the end of the 19th century. Harnack tries to bring Jesus into the contemporary world; Schweitzer insists that he was "a Jew of the First Century." He is strange to us. We can understand his life only so far as we enter into the Apocalyptic conceptions of the Kingdom of God which dominated his thought. Since Johannes Weiss and Schweitzer, New Testament scholars have been grappling with the Apocalyptic problem.

Any complete account of the change in theological thought since 1900 would include the contribution of Rudolf Otto and his *Idea of the Holy* which, with its emphasis on the "irrational" element in religion, was one of the signs of the movement away from the Liberal Protestant position. We must, however, concentrate attention on the most remarkable feature of the period —the return to dogmatic theology. We have seen how Harnack and his fellow "liberals" looked forward to the fading of dogma and the relaxing of the doctrinal authority of the Church. Precisely the opposite happened. The crisis of civilisation was inevitably also a crisis for the Christian faith, and in the stress of conflict those Churches, and groups within the Churches, which held most firmly to the confession of faith and the discipline of the ecclesiastical organisation proved the best equipped to meet the storm. In Germany it was those Lutherans who adhered to the "Confession" who resisted the designs of Hitler and his neo-pagan cult; while in the conflict with atheistic Communism the power of dogma and discipline was once more demonstrated. Just as in the early Church, pressure from without of persecution and opposing doctrines led once more to a need for clear definition of what Christianity stood for and for the closing of the ranks of believers.

Karl Barth is the outstanding personality of this movement. In him we have the greatest systematic Protestant theologian of modern times. A convert from Liberal Protestantism, he is engaged upon a massive work in many volumes on the doctrine of the Word of God in which he is producing a Biblical theology that aims at being a restatement of the Reformation doctrines. In Barth and his followers we find no search for the historical Jesus, nor do we find any recourse to philosophy. The theological task, as Barth understands it, is to draw out and set in order the Biblical revelation, and this without regard to any alleged revelations other than the word of God found through the Bible. It must be added that Barth, throughout, claims to be writing and thinking in and for the Church, without which his activity would be meaningless. Not all modern Biblical theology is in agreement with Barth, but on the whole it accepts his view of the nature of theology and in this respect is out of sympathy with Harnack's quest for the historical Jesus.

We may say, then, that Harnack is "outmoded" in the sense that interest has, for the time, shifted from the problem which he tried to solve, and also in the sense that probably no scholar to-day who attempted to answer his question would be satisfied with all his conclusions. Does this imply that Harnack's lectures are of merely historical interest and of no value to the student of Christian origins? We should be mistaken if we thought so, for to be "outmoded" is by no means the same as to be refuted and every one of his main contentions can be defended. If, in the end, we decide, as I think we must, that he has not given the final answer to the question What is Christianity? we shall learn much from him and not least by the stimulus which he gives by challenging us to inquire why he fails to satisfy us. We have the reflections of a great scholar and a man of acute and devout mind on a subject of monumentous importance—they do not become negligible because they are out of fashion.

Can it truly be alleged that Harnack and others who sought for "the historical Jesus" and attached importance to "the religion of Jesus," as distinct from the religion centred upon Jesus, were attempting something that was either unnecessary or impossible? I think not : To arrive at some knowledge of the person who was called Jesus of Nazareth is not in itself an obviously hopeless enterprise. We may note that many simple persons who read the Gospels do at least seem to gather from them a distinct picture of the man. In spite of the discrepancies and various points of view of the records, the figure of Jesus is not to them either vague or indistinct. Such readers recognise an authentic and individual voice, which is not the voice of tradition but of him who makes the tradition worthy of attention. It cannot be an altogether futile aim for scholarship to pursue this and to inquire why the impression is made, to disengage, as it were, the person from the accretions and, perhaps, distortions which tradition may have brought and to trace the Church's memories back to the source in the actual life and words of the Lord. Harnack was not trying to do the impossible. He failed, I think, because he was unduly sceptical about the tradition, and because he was too much a child of 19th-century rationalism. He took too narrow a view of the power of Spirit and was afraid of all that savoured of the super-normal or "miraculous." The Apocalyptic ideas to him were simply mistaken and, unlike ourselves, he did not see that the Kingdom of God may come through catastrophe. In my opinion, basing ourselves on the Gospel of Mark, we may have a coherent idea of the ministry of Jesus and, what is more important, of his experience and its development from the baptism by John to the crucifixion. Further, it seems to me, that this experience is congruous with what the earliest traditions, including St. Paul, have to say about Jesus as Lord and Saviour.

Surely it is a paradox to say that the knowledge of Jesus, as he was in his lifetime, is of no importance. I do not see how anyone who believes in the Incarnation could make such an assertion. If he were, like the Buddha, only a teacher of a "way" one could quite consistently hold that the personality of the teacher is irrelevant. If the teaching is true, it matters little who the teacher was. But Christianity is a religion centred upon a person, who is believed to be the supreme revelation of God, one who not only speaks the words of God, but is himself the Word of God. It would be strange indeed if we had only dim and fragmentary information of what he was.

Thus we must be grateful to Harnack for his earnest endeavour to know the historical Jesus and for the light which

he throws on some aspects of the Lord Christ. We may accept
very much of his picture, but we are left asking, Is there not
more? Is the Jesus of Harnack the Christ of Christian experience? There is indeed much more. The reading of Harnack's
essay on *What is Christianity?* may perhaps be the beginning
and not the end of a quest for the real Jesus Christ.

LONDON   1958   W. R. M.

LECTURE ONE

THE GREAT English philosopher John Stuart Mill has somewhere observed that mankind cannot be too often reminded that there was once a man of the name of Socrates. That is true; but still more important is it to remind mankind again and again that a man of the name of Jesus Christ once stood in their midst. The fact, of course, has been brought home to us from our youth up; but unhappily it cannot be said that public instruction in our time is calculated to preserve the image of Jesus Christ for us in any impressive way, and as an inalienable possession after our schooldays are over and for our whole life. And even though no one who has once absorbed a ray of Christ's light can ever again become as though he had never heard of him; even though in the depths of every soul that has been once touched an impression may remain, still a confused recollection of this kind, which is often only a "superstition," is not enough to give strength and life. Should the desire, however, for further and more trustworthy knowledge about him arise, and a man want positive information as to who Jesus Christ was, and as to the real purport of his message, he no sooner asks for it than he finds himself, if he consults the literature of the day, surrounded by a clatter of contradictory voices. He hears some people maintaining that primitive Christianity was closely akin to Buddhism, and he is accordingly told that it is in fleeing the world and in pessimism that the sublime character of this religion and its profound meaning are revealed. Others, on the contrary, assure him that Christianity is an optimistic religion, and that it must be thought of simply and solely as a higher phase of Judaism; and they, too, also suppose that in saying this they have said something very profound. Others, again, maintain the opposite; they assert that the Gospel did away with Judaism, and that it itself

originated under Greek influences of mysterious operation, and
is to be understood as a blossom on the tree of Hellenism.
Religious philosophers come forward and declare that the metaphysical system which, as they say, was developed out of the
Gospel, is its real kernel and the revelation of its secret; but
others reply that the Gospel has nothing to do with philosophy,
that it was meant for feeling and suffering humanity, and that
philosophy has only been forced upon it. Finally, the newest
critics of all step into the field and assure us that the whole history of religion, morality and philosophy is nothing but clothes
and finery; that what at all times underlies them, as the only
real motive power, is the history of economics; that accordingly
Christianity, too, was in its origin nothing more than a social
movement and Christ a social deliverer—the deliverer of the
oppressed lower classes.

It is somewhat touching to observe how anxious everyone is
to rediscover himself, together with his own point of view and
his own circle of interest, in this Jesus Christ, or at least to get
a share in him. It is the perennial repetition of the spectacle
which was seen even as early as the second century in the
"Gnostic" movement, and which takes the form of a struggle,
on the part of every conceivable tendency of thought, for the
possession of Jesus Christ. Why, quite recently, not only, I think,
Tolstoi's ideas, but even Nietzsche's have been exhibited in their
special affinity with the Gospel; and there is perhaps more to be
said even upon this subject that is worth attention than upon
the connexion between a good deal of "theological" and "philosophical" speculation and Christ's teaching.

But nevertheless, when taken together, the impression which
these contradictory opinions convey is disheartening : the confusion seems hopeless. How can we take it amiss of anyone if,
after trying to find out how the question stands, he gives it up?
Perhaps he may go further, and declare that after all the question does not matter. How are we concerned with events that
happened, or with a person who lived, nineteen hundred years
ago? We must look for our ideals and our strength to the
present; to evolve them laboriously out of old manuscripts is a
fantastic proceeding that can lead nowhere. The man who so

speaks is not wrong; but neither is he right. What we are and what we possess, in any high sense, we possess from the past and by the past—only so much of it, of course, as has had results and makes its influence felt up to the present day. To acquire a sound knowledge of the past is the business and the duty, not only of the historian but also of every one who wishes to make the wealth and the strength so gained his own. But that the Gospel is a part of this past which nothing else can replace has been affirmed again and again by the greatest minds. "Let intellectual and spiritual culture progress, and the human mind expand, as much as it will; beyond the grandeur and the moral elevation of Christianity, as it sparkles and shines in the Gospels, the human mind will not advance." So spoke Goethe, after making many experiments and labouring indefatigably at himself; so it was that he summed up the result to which his moral and historical insight led him. Even though we were to feel no desire on our own part, it would still be worth while, because of this man's testimony, to devote our serious attention to what he came to regard as so precious; and if, contrary to his declaration, louder and more confident voices are heard to-day, proclaiming that the Christian religion has outlived itself, let us accept this as an invitation to make a closer acquaintance with the religion whose certificate of death people suppose that they can already exhibit.

But in truth this religion and the efforts which it evokes are more active to-day than they used to be. We may say to the credit of our age that it takes an eager interest in the problem of the nature and value of Christianity, and that there is more study and inquiry in regard to this subject now than was the case thirty years ago. Even in the attempts that people make to feel their way in it, the strange and abstruse replies that are given to questions, the manner in which it is caricatured, the chaotic confusion which it exhibits, nay, even in the hatred that it excites, a real life and an earnest endeavour may be traced. Only do not let us suppose that there is anything exemplary in this endeavour, and that we are the first to shake off an authoritative religion and struggle after one that shall really make us free and be of independent growth—a struggle which must of necessity give rise to much confusion and half-truth. Sixty-two years ago Carlyle wrote: "In these distracted times, when the Religious Principle, driven out of most Churches, either lies unseen in the hearts of good men, looking and longing and silently working there towards some new Revelation; or else wanders homeless over the world, like a disembodied soul seeking its terrestrial organisation,—into how many strange shapes, of Superstition and Fanaticism, does it not tentatively and errantly cast itself! The higher Enthusiasm of man's nature is for the while without Exponent; yet does it continue indestructible, unweariedly active, and work blindly in the great chaotic deep: thus Sect after Sect, and Church after Church, bodies itself forth, and melts again into new metamorphosis."

No one who understands the times in which we live can deny that these words sound as if they had been written to-day. But it is not with "the religious principle" and the ways in which it has developed that we are going to concern ourselves in these lectures. We shall try to answer the more modest but not less pressing question, What is Christianity? What was it? What has it become? The answer to this question may, we hope, also throw light by the way on the more comprehensive one, What is Religion, and what ought it to be to us? In dealing with religion, is it not after all with the Christian religion alone that we have to do? Other religions no longer stir the depths of our hearts.

What is Christianity? It is solely in its historical sense that we shall try to answer this question here; that is to say, we shall employ the methods of historical science and the experience of life gained by witnessing the actual course of history. We thus exclude the view of the question taken by the apologist and the religious philosopher. On this point permit me to say a few words.

Apologetics holds a necessary place in religious knowledge, and to demonstrate the validity of the Christian religion and exhibit its importance for the moral and intellectual life is a great and a worthy undertaking. But it is one which must not be confounded with the purely historical question as to the

nature of that religion, or else historical research will be brought
into complete discredit. Moreover, in the kind of apologetics
that is now required no really high standard has as yet been set.
Apart from a few steps that have been taken in the direction of
improvement, this whole subject of study is in a deplorable state :
it is not clear as to the positions to be defended, and it is uncertain as to the means to be employed. It is also not infrequently
pursued in an undignified and obtrusive fashion. Apologists
imagine that they are doing a great work by crying up religion
as though it were a job-lot at a sale, or a universal remedy for
all social ills. They are perpetually snatching, too, at all sorts of
baubles, so as to make religion cut a fine figure. In their
endeavour to present it as a glorious necessity, they deprive it
of its earnest character, and at the best only prove that it is
something which may be safely accepted because it can do no
harm. Finally, they cannot refrain from slipping in some Church
programme of yesterday, and "demonstrating" its claims as
well; for the structure of their ideas is so loose that an idea or
two more makes no difference. The mischief that has been
thereby done already and is still being done is indescribable.
No! the Christian religion is something simple and sublime; it
means one thing and one thing only : Eternal life in the midst
of time, by the strength and under the eyes of God. It is no
ethical or social *arcanum* for the preservation or improvement
of things generally. To make what it has done for civilisation
and human progress the main question, and to determine its
value by the answer, is to do it violence at the start. Goethe
once said, "Mankind is always advancing, and man always
remains the same." It is to *man* that religion pertains—to man,
as one who in the midst of all change and progress himself never
changes. Christian apologetics must recognise, then, that it is
with religion in its simple nature and its simple strength that it
has to do. Religion, to be sure, does not exist for itself alone; it
lives in an inner fellowship with all the activities of the mind
and with moral and economical conditions as well. But it is
emphatically not a mere function or an exponent of them; it is
a mighty power that sets to work of itself, hindering or further-
ing, destroying or making fruitful. The main thing is to learn

what religion is and in what its essential character consists—no
matter what position the individual who examines it may take
up in regard to it, or whether in his own life he values it or not.

But the point of view of the philosophical theorist, in the strict
sense of the word, will also find no place in these lectures. Had
they been delivered sixty years ago, it would have been our
endeavour to arrive by speculative reasoning at some general
conception of religion, and then try to define the Christian
religion accordingly. But we have rightly become sceptical about
the value of this procedure. *Latet dolus in generalibus.* We know
to-day that life cannot be spanned by general conceptions, and
that there is no general conception of religion to which actual
religions are related simply and solely as species to genus. Nay,
the question may even be asked whether there is any such
generic conception as "religion" at all. Is the common element
in it anything more than a vague disposition? Is it only an
empty spot in our innermost being that the word denotes, which
every one fills up in a different fashion, and many do not per-
ceive at all? I am not of this opinion; I am convinced, rather,
that at bottom we have to do here with something which is
common to us all, and which in the course of history has
struggled up out of torpor and discord into unity and light. I
am convinced that Augustine is right when he says, "Thou,
Lord, hast made us for Thyself, and our heart is restless until it
finds rest in Thee." But to prove this is so; to exhibit the nature
and the claims of religion by psychological analysis, including
the psychology of peoples, is not the task that we shall undertake in what follows. We shall keep to the purely historical
theme. What is the Christian religion?

Where are we to look for our materials? The answer seems
to be simple and at the same time exhaustive : *Jesus Christ and
his Gospel.* But however little doubt there may be that this must
form not only our point of departure but also the matter with
which our investigations will mainly deal, it is equally certain
that we must not be content to exhibit the mere image of Jesus
Christ and the main features of his Gospel. We must not be
content to stop there, because every great and powerful personality reveals a part of what it is only when seen in those

whom it influences. Nay, it may be said that the more powerful
the personality which a man possesses, and the more he takes
hold of the inner life of others, the less can the sum-total of
what he is be known only by what he himself says and does.
We must look at the reflection and the effects which he produced in those whose leader and master he became. That is why
a complete answer to the question What is Christianity? is
impossible so long as we are restricted to Jesus Christ's teaching
alone. We must include the first generation of his disciples as
well—those who ate and drank with him—and we must listen
to what they tell us of the effect which he had upon their
lives.

But even this does not exhaust our materials. If Christianity
is an example of a great power valid not for one particular
epoch alone; if in and through it, not once only, but again and
again, great forces have been disengaged, we must include all
the latter products of its spirit. It is not a question of a "doctrine" being handed down by uniform repetition or arbitrarily
distorted; it is a question of a *life*, again and again kindled
afresh, and now burning with a flame of its own. We may also
add that Christ himself and the apostles were convinced that the
religion which they were planting would in the ages to come
have a greater destiny and a deeper meaning than it possessed
at the time of its institution; they trusted to its spirit leading
from one point of light to another and developing higher forces.
Just as we cannot obtain a complete knowledge of a tree without regarding not only its root and its stem but also its bark, its
branches, and the way in which it blooms, so we cannot form
any right estimate of the Christian religion unless we take our
stand upon a comprehensive induction that shall cover all the
facts of its history. It is true that Christianity has had its classical epoch; nay more, it had a founder who himself was what
he taught—to steep ourselves in him is still the chief matter; but
to restrict ourselves to him means to take a point of view too
low for his significance. Individual religious life was what he
wanted to kindle and what he did kindle; it is, as we shall see,
his peculiar greatness to have led men to God, so that they may
thenceforth live their own life with Him. How, then, can we be

silent about the history of the Gospel if we wish to know what he was?

It may be objected that put in this way the problem is too difficult, and that its solution threatens to be accompanied by many errors and defects. That is not to be denied; but to state a problem in easier terms, that is to say in this case inaccurately, because of the difficulties surrounding it, would be a very perverse expedient. Moreover, even though the difficulties increase, the work is, on the other hand, facilitated by the problem being stated in a larger manner; for it helps us to grasp what is *essential* in the phenomena, and to distinguish kernel and husk.

Jesus Christ and his disciples were situated in their day just as we are situated in ours; that is to say, their feelings, their thoughts, their judgments and their efforts were bounded by the horizon and the framework in which their own nation was set and by its condition at the time. Had it been otherwise, they would not have been men of flesh and blood, but mere spectres. For seventeen hundred years, indeed, people thought, and many among us still think, that the "humanity" of Jesus Christ, which is a part of their creed, is sufficiently provided for by the assumption that he had a human body and a human soul. As if it were possible to have that without having any definite character as an individual! To be a man means, in the first place, to possess a certain mental and spiritual disposition, determined in such and such a way, and thereby limited and circumscribed; and, in the second place, it means to be situated, with this disposition, in a historical environment which in its turn is also limited and circumscribed. Anything beyond this means to be not "a man." It at once follows, then, that no one can think, speak or do anything at all without his peculiar disposition and his own age coming in as factors. A single word may seem to be really classical and valid for all time, and yet the very *language* in which it is spoken gives it very palpable limitations. Much less is a spiritual personality, as a whole, susceptible of being represented in a way that will banish the feeling of its limitations, and with those limitations, the sense of something strange or conventional; and this feeling must necessarily be enhanced the farther in point of time the spectator is removed.

From these circumstances it follows that the historian, whose business and highest duty it is to determine what is of permanent value, is of necessity required not to cleave to words but *to find out what is essential*. The "whole" Christ, the "whole" Gospel, if we mean by this motto the external image taken in all its details and set up for imitation, is just as bad and deceptive a shibboleth as the "whole" Luther, and the like. It is bad because it enslaves us, and it is deceptive because the people who proclaim it do not think of taking it seriously, and could not do so if they tried. They cannot do so because they cannot cease to feel, understand and judge as children of their age.

There are only two possibilities here : either the Gospel is in all respects identical with its earliest form, in which case it came with its time, and with its time has departed; or else it contains something which, under differing historical forms, is of permanent validity. The latter is the true view. The history of the Church shows us in its very commencement that "primitive Christianity" had to disappear in order that "Christianity" might remain; and in the same way in later ages one metamorphosis followed upon another. From the beginning it was a question of getting rid of formulas, correcting expectations, altering ways of feeling, and this is a process to which there is no end. But by the very fact that our survey embraces the whole course as well as the inception, we enhance our standard of what is essential and of real value.

We enhance our standard—but we need not wait to take it from the history of those later ages. The thing itself reveals it. We shall see that the Gospel in the Gospel is something so simple, something that speaks to us with so much power, that it cannot easily be mistaken. Comprehensive and methodical directions and general introductions are unnecessary to enable us to find the way to it. No one who possesses a fresh eye for what is alive, and true feeling for what is really great, can fail to see it and distinguish it from its contemporary integument. And even though there may be many individual aspects of it where the task of distinguishing what is permanent from what is fleeting, what is rudimentary from what is merely historical, is not quite easy, we must not be like the child who, wanting to

get at the kernel of a bulb, went on picking off the leaves until
there was nothing left, and in the end could not help seeing that
it was just the leaves that made the bulb. Endeavours of this
kind are not unknown in the history of the Christian religion,
but they are thrown into the shade by others which seek to convince us that there is no such thing as either kernel or husk,
growth or decay, but that everything is of equal value and alike
permanent.

In these lectures, then, we shall deal first of all with the
Gospel of Jesus Christ, and this theme will occupy the greater
part of our attention. We shall then show what impression he
himself and his Gospel made upon the first generation of his
disciples. Finally, we shall follow the leading changes which the
Christian idea has undergone in the course of history, and try
to recognise its chief types. What is common to all the forms
which it has taken, corrected by reference to the Gospel, and,
conversely, the chief features of the Gospel, corrected
by reference to history, will, we may be allowed to hope,
bring us to the kernel of the matter. Within the limits of a short
series of lectures it is, of course, only to what is important that
attention can be called; but perhaps there will be no disadvantage in fixing our attention, for once, only on the strong lines
and prominent points of the relief, and, with everything secondary put into the background, looking at the vast material in a
concentrated form. We shall even refrain, and permissibly refrain, from enlarging, by way of introduction, on Judaism and
its external and internal relations, and on the Græco-Roman
world. We must never, of course, wholly shut our eyes to them
—nay, we must always keep them in mind; but we need not go
into them at any great length. Jesus Christ's teaching will at
once bring us by steps which, if few, will be large, to a height
where its connexion with Judaism will appear only a loose one,
and most of the threads leading from it into "contemporary
history" become of no importance at all. This may seem a
paradoxical thing to say; for just now we are being
earnestly assured, with an air as though it were some new
discovery that was being imparted to us, that Jesus Christ's
teaching cannot be understood, nay, cannot be accurately

represented, except by having regard to its connexion with the Jewish doctrines prevalent at the time, and by first of all setting them out in full. There is much that is true in this statement, and yet, as we shall see, it is incorrect. It becomes absolutely false, however, when worked up into the dazzling thesis that the Gospel is intelligible only as the religion of a despairing section of the Jewish nation; that it was the last effort of a decadent age, driven by distress into a renunciation of this earth, and then trying to storm heaven and demanding civic rights there— a religion of miserabilism! It is rather remarkable that the really desperate were just those who did not welcome it, but fought against it; remarkable that its leaders, so far as we know them, do not, in fact, bear any of the marks of sickly despair; most remarkable of all, that while indeed renouncing the world and its goods, they establish, in love and holiness, a brotherly union which declares war on the world's misery. The oftener I re-read and consider the Gospels, the more do I find that the contemporary discords, in the midst of which the Gospel stood, and out of which it arose, sink into the background. I entertain no doubt that even the founder had an eye to *man* in whatever external situation he might be found —*man* who, at bottom, always remains the same, whether he be moving upwards or downwards, whether he be in riches or poverty, whether he be of strong mind or of weak. It is the consciousness of all these oppositions being ultimately beneath it, and of its own place above them, that gives the Gospel its sovereignty; for in every man it looks to the point that is unaffected by all these differences. This is very clear in Paul's case; he dominates all earthly things and circumstances like a king, and desires to see them so dominated. The thesis of the decadent age and the religion of the wretched may serve to lead us into the outer court; it may even correctly point to that which originally gave the Gospel its form; but if it is offered us as a key for the understanding of this religion in itself, we must reject it. Moreover, this thesis and the pretensions which it makes are only illustrations of a fashion which has become general in the writing of history, and which in that province will naturally have a longer reign than other fashions, because by its means light can, in fact, be thrown upon much that was obscure. But its devotees do not get at the kernel, assuming, as they silently do, that no such kernel exists.

Let me conclude this lecture by touching briefly on one other important point. In history absolute judgments are impossible. This is a truth which in these days—I say advisedly, in these days,—is clear and incontestable. History can only show how things have been; and even where we can throw light upon the past, and understand and criticise it, we must not presume to think that by any process of abstraction absolute judgments as to the value to be assigned to past events can be obtained from the results of a purely historical survey. Such judgments are the creation only of feeling and of will; they are a subjective act. The false notion that the understanding can produce them is a heritage of that protracted epoch in which knowing and knowledge were expected to accomplish everything; in which it was believed that they could be stretched so as to be capable of covering and satisfying all the needs of the mind and the heart. That they cannot do. This is a truth which, in many an hour of ardent work, falls heavily upon our soul, and yet—what a hopeless thing it would be for mankind if the higher peace to which it aspires, and the clearness, the certainty and the strength for which it strives, were dependent on the measure of its learning and its knowledge.

LECTURE TWO

OUR FIRST section deals with *the main features of the message delivered by Jesus Christ*. In these is also included the way in which he delivered his message. We shall see how essential a part of his character is here exhibited, for "he spoke as one having authority and not as the Scribes." But before describing these features I feel it my duty to tell you briefly how matters stand in regard to the sources of our knowledge.

Apart from some important information given by the apostle Paul, our authorities for the message which Jesus Christ delivered are the first three Gospels. Everything that we know, independently of these Gospels, about Jesus' history and his teaching, may be easily put on a small sheet of paper, so little does it come to. In particular, the fourth Gospel, which does not emanate or profess to emanate from the apostle John, cannot be taken as a historical authority in the ordinary meaning of the word. The author of it acted with sovereign freedom, transposed events and put them in a new light, drew up the discourses himself, and illustrated great thoughts by imaginary situations. Although, therefore, his work is not altogether devoid of a real, if scarcely recognisable, traditional element, it can hardly make any claim to be considered an authority for Jesus' history; only little of what he says can be accepted, and that little with caution. On the other hand, it is an authority of the first rank for answering the question, What vivid views of Jesus' person, what kind of light and warmth, did the Gospel disengage?

Sixty years ago David Friedrich Strauss thought that he had almost entirely destroyed the historical credibility not only of the fourth but also of the first three Gospels as well. The historical criticism of two generations has succeeded in restoring that credibility in its main outlines. These Gospels are not, it is true, historical works any more than the fourth; they were not written with the simple object of giving the facts as they were; they are books composed for the work of evangelisation. Their purpose is to awaken a belief in Jesus Christ's person and mission; and the purpose is served by the description of his deeds and discourses, as well as by the references to the Old Testament. Nevertheless they are not useless as sources of history, more especially as the object with which they were written is not supplied from without, but coincides in part with what Jesus intended. Such other great leading purposes, however, as have been ascribed to the evangelists have one and all proved unfounded, although with each individual evangelist many secondary purposes may have come into play. The Gospels are not "party tracts"; neither are they writings which as yet bear the radical impress of the Greek spirit. In their essential substance they belong to the first, the Jewish, epoch of Christianity, that brief epoch which may be denoted as the palæontological. That we possess any reports dating from that time, even though, as is obvious in the first and third Gospels, the setting and composition are by another hand, is one of those historical arrangements for which we cannot be too thankful. Criticism to-day universally recognises the unique character of the Gospels. What especially marks them off from all subsequent literature is the way in which they tell their story. This species of literary art, which took shape partly by analogy with the didactic narratives of the Jews, and partly from catechetical necessities—this simple and impressive form of exposition was, even a few decades later, no longer capable of reproduction. From the time that the Gospel was transferred to the broad ground of the Græco-Roman world it appropriated the literary forms of the Greeks, and the style of the evangelists was then felt to be something strange but sublime. But when all is said, the Greek language lies upon these writings only like a diaphanous veil, and it requires hardly any effort to retranslate their contents into Hebrew or Aramaic. That the tradition here presented to us is, in the main, at first hand, is obvious.

How fixed was this tradition in point of form is proved by the third Gospel. It was composed by a Greek, probably in the time of Domitian; and in the second part of his work, the Acts of the Apostles, he shows, what he had already shown in the preface to the first, that he was familiar with the literary language of his nation and that he was an excellent master of style. But in the Gospel narrative he did not dare to abandon the traditional type; he tells his story in the same style as Mark and Matthew, with the same connexion of sentences, the same colour, nay, in many cases with the same details; it is only the ruder words and expressions, which would offend literary taste, that are sparingly corrected. There is another aspect, too, in which his Gospel strikes us as remarkable : he assures us at the beginning of it that he has "had perfect understanding of all things from the very first," and has examined many accounts. But if we test him by his authorities, we find that he has kept in the main to Mark's Gospel, and to a source which we also find appearing again in Matthew. These accounts both seemed to him, as a respectable chronicler, to be preferable to the crowd of others. That offers a good guarantee for them. No historian has found that it is possible or necessary to substitute any other tradition for the one which we have here.

Another point : this tradition is, apart from the story of the Passion, almost exclusively Galilean in its character. Had not the history of Jesus' public activity been really governed by this geographical horizon, tradition could not have so described it; for every historical narrative with an eye to effect would have represented him as working chiefly in Jerusalem. That is the account given by the fourth Gospel. That our first three evangelists almost entirely refrain from saying anything about Jerusalem arouses "a good prejudice" in their favour.

It is true that, measured by the standard of "agreement, inspiration and completeness," these writings leave a very great deal to be desired, and even when judged by a more human standard they suffer from not a few imperfections. Rude additions from a later age they do not, indeed, exhibit—it will always remain a noteworthy fact that, conversely, it is only the fourth Gospel which makes Greeks ask after Jesus—but still they, too, reflect, here and there, the circumstances in which the primitive Christian community was placed and the experiences which it afterwards underwent. People nowadays, however, resort to such explanations more readily than is necessary. Further, the conviction that Old Testament prophecy was fulfilled in Jesus' history had a disturbing effect on tradition. Lastly, in some of the narratives the miraculous element is obviously intensified. On the other hand, Strauss' contention that the Gospels contain a very great deal that is mythical has not been borne out, even if the very indefinite and defective conception of what "mythical" means in Strauss' application of the word be allowed to pass. It is almost exclusively in the account of Jesus' childhood, and there only sparingly, that a mythical touch can be traced. None of these disturbing elements affect the heart of the narrative; not a few of them easily lend themselves to correction, partly by a comparison of the Gospels one with another, partly through the sound judgment that is matured by historical study.

But the miraculous element, all these reports of miracles! Not Strauss only, but many others too, have allowed themselves to be frightened by them into roundly denying the credibility of the Gospels. But, on the other hand, historical science in this last generation has taken a great step in advance by learning to pass a more intelligent and benevolent judgment on those narratives, and accordingly even reports of the marvellous can now be counted amongst the materials of history and turned to good account. I owe it to you and to the subject briefly to specify the position which historical science to-day takes up in regard to these reports.

In the first place, we know that Gospels come from a time in which the marvellous may be said to have been something of almost daily occurrence. People felt and saw that they were surrounded by wonders, and not by any means only in the religious sphere. Certain spiritualists among us excepted, we are now accustomed to associate the question of miracles exclusively with the question of religion. In those days it was otherwise. The fountains of the marvellous were many, but while some sort of divinity was, of course, supposed to be at work in every case —it was a god who accomplished the miracle—it was not to every god that people stood in a religious relation. Further, in those days, the strict conception which we now attach to the word "miracle" was yet unknown; it came in only with a knowledge of the laws of Nature and their general validity. Before that, no sound insight existed into what was possible and what was impossible, what was rule and what was exception. But where this distinction is not clear, or where, as the case may be, the question has never been raised at all in any rigorous form, there are no such things as miracles in the strict sense of the word. No one can feel anything to be an interruption of the order of Nature who does not yet know what the order of Nature is. Miracles, then, could not possess the significance for that age which, if they existed, they would possess for ours. For that age all wonders were only extraordinary events, and, even if they formed a world by themselves, it was certain that there were countless points in which that other world mysteriously encroached upon our own. Nor was it only God's messengers, but magicians and charlatans as well, who were thought to be possessed of some of these miraculous powers. The significance attaching to "miracles" was, therefore, in those days a subject of never-ending controversy: at one moment a high value was set upon them and they were considered to belong to the very essence of religion; at another, they were spoken of with contempt.

In the second place, we now know that eminent persons have not to wait until they have been long dead, or even for several years, to have miracles reported of them; they are reported at once, often the very next day. The habit of condemning a narrative, or of ascribing it to a later age, only because it includes stories of miracles, is a piece of prejudice.

In the third place, we are firmly convinced that what happens in space and time is subject to the general laws of motion, and that in this sense, as an interruption of the order of Nature, there can be no such things as "miracles." But we also recognise that the religious man—if religion really permeates him and is something more than a belief in the religion of others—is certain that he is not shut up within a blind and brutal course of Nature, but that this course of Nature serves higher ends, or, as it may be, that some inner and divine power can help us so to encounter it as that "everything must necessarily be for the best." This experience, which I might express in one word as the ability to escape from the power and the service of transitory

things, is always felt afresh to be a miracle each time that it
occurs; it is inseparable from every higher religion, and were it
to be surrendered religion would be at an end. But it is an
experience which is as true of the life of the individual as it is
of the great course of human history. How clearly and logically,
then, must a religious man think, if, in spite of this experience,
he holds firmly to the inviolable character of what happens in
space and time. Who can wonder that even great minds fail to
keep the two spheres quite separate? And as we all live, first and
foremost, in the domain, not of ideas but of perceptions, and in
a language of metaphor, how can we avoid conceiving what is
divine and what makes us free as a mighty power working upon
the order of Nature, and breaking through or arresting it? This
notion, though it belong only to the realm of fantasy and metaphor, will, it seems, last as long as religion itself.

In the fourth place, and lastly, although the order of Nature
be inviolable, we are not yet by any means acquainted with all
the forces working in it and acting reciprocally with other forces.
Our acquaintance even with the forces inherent in matter, and
with the field of their action, is incomplete; while of psychic
forces we know very much less. We see that a strong will and
a firm faith exert an influence upon the life of the body, and
produce phenomena which strike us as marvellous. Has anyone
ever yet drawn any sure line between the spheres of the possible
and the actual? Who can say how far the influence of soul
upon soul and of soul upon body reaches? No one. Who can
still maintain that any extraordinary phenomenon that may
appear in this domain is entirely based on error and delusion?
Miracles, it is true, do not happen; but of the marvellous and
the inexplicable there is no lack. In our present state of knowledge we have become more careful, more hesitating in our
judgment, in regard to the stories of the miraculous which we
have received from antiquity. That the earth in its course stood
still; that a she-ass spoke; that a storm was quieted by a word,
we do not believe, and we shall never again believe; but that the
lame walked, the blind saw and the deaf heard will not be so
summarily dismissed as an illusion.

From these suggestions you can arrive for yourselves at the

right position to take up in regard to the miraculous stories related in the Gospels, and at their net result. In particular cases —that is to say, in the application of general principles to concrete statements—some uncertainty will always remain. So far as I can judge, the stories may be grouped as follows: (1) Stories which had their origin in an exaggerated view of natural events of an impressive character; (2) stories which had their origin in sayings or parables, or in the projection of inner experiences on to the external world; (3) stories such as arose in the interest of seeing Old Testament sayings fulfilled; (4) stories of surprising cures effected by Jesus' spiritual force; (5) stories of which we cannot fathom the secret. It is very remarkable, however, that Jesus himself did not assign that critical importance to his miraculous deeds which even the evangelist Mark and the others all attributed to them. Did he not exclaim, in tones of complaint and accusation, "Unless ye see signs and wonders, ye will not believe"? He who uttered these words cannot have held that belief in the wonders which he wrought was the right or the only avenue to the recognition of his person and his mission; nay, in all essential points he must have thought of them quite otherwise than his evangelists. And the remarkable fact that these very evangelists, without appreciating its range, hand down the statement that Jesus "did not many mighty works there because of their unbelief," shows us, from another and a different side, with what caution we must receive these miraculous stories, and into what category we must put them.

It follows from all this that if we want to evade the Gospel we must not entrench ourselves behind the miraculous stories related by the evangelists. In spite of those stories, nay, in part even in them, we are presented with a reality which has claims upon our attention. Study it, and do not let yourselves be deterred because this or that miraculous story strikes you as strange or leaves you cold. If there is anything here that you find unintelligible, put it quietly aside. Perhaps you will have to leave it there for ever; perhaps the meaning will dawn upon you later and the story assume a significance of which you never dreamt. Once more let me say: Do not be deterred. The question of miracles is of relative indifference in comparison with everything else which is to be found in the Gospels. It is not miracles that matter; the question on which everything turns is whether we are helplessly yoked to an inexorable necessity, or whether a God exists who rules and governs, and whose power to compel Nature we can move by prayer and make a part of our experience.

Our evangelists, as we know, do not tell us anything about the history of Jesus' early development; they tell us only of his public activity. Two of the Gospels do, it is true, contain an introductory history (the history of Jesus' birth), but we may disregard it; for even if it contained something more trustworthy than it does actually contain, it would be as good as useless for our purpose. That is to say, the evangelists themselves never refer to it, nor make Jesus himself refer to his antecedents. On the contrary, they tell us that Jesus' mother and his brethren were completely surprised at his coming forward, and did not know what to make of it. Paul, too, is silent; so that we can be sure that the oldest tradition knew nothing of any stories of Jesus' birth.

We know nothing of Jesus' history for the first thirty years of his life. Is there not a terrible uncertainty here? What is there left us if we have to begin our task by confessing that we are unable to write any life of Jesus? How can we write the history of a man of whose development we know nothing, and with only a year or two of whose life we are acquainted? Well, however certain it may be that our materials are insufficient for a "biography," they are very weighty in other respects, and even their silence on the first thirty years is instructive. They are weighty because they give us information upon three important points : *In the first place, they offer us a plain picture of Jesus' teaching, in regard both to its main features and to its individual application; in the second place, they tell us how his life issued in the service of his vocation; and in the third place, they describe to us the impression which he made upon his disciples, and which they transmitted.*

Here, indeed, we have three very important points; nay, they are the points on which everything turns. It is because we can get a clear view of them that a characteristic picture of Jesus is possible; or, to speak more modestly, that there is some hope for an attempt to understand what his aims were, what he was, and what he signifies for us.

As regards the thirty years of silence, we gather from our evangelists that Jesus did not think it necessary to give his disciples any information about them. But much may be said about them negatively. First of all, it is very improbable that he went through any Rabbinical school; he nowhere speaks like a man who had assimilated any theological culture of a technical kind, or learned the art of scholarly exegesis. Compare him in this respect with the apostle Paul; how clearly it can be seen from the latter's epistles that he had sat at the feet of theological teachers. With Jesus we find nothing of the kind; and hence he caused a stir by appearing in the schools and teaching at all. He lived and had his being in the sacred writings, but not after the manner of a professional teacher.

Neither can he have had any relations with the Essenes, a remarkable order of Jewish monks. Were that so, he would have been one of those pupils who show their dependence on their teachers by proclaiming and doing the opposite of what they have been taught. The Essenes made a point of the most extreme purity in the eye of the law, and held severely aloof not only from the impure but even from those who were a little lax in their purity. It is only thus that we can understand their living strictly apart, their dwelling in particular places, and their practice of frequent ablutions every day. Jesus exhibits a complete contrast with this mode of life : he goes in search of sinners and eats with them. So fundamental a difference alone makes it certain that he had nothing to do with the Essenes. His aims and the means which he employed divide him off from them. If he appears to coincide with them in many of his individual injunctions to his disciples, these are accidental points of contact, as his motives were quite other than theirs.

Further, unless all appearances are deceptive, no stormy crisis, no breach with his past, lies behind the period of Jesus' life that we know. In none of his sayings or discourses, whether he is threatening and punishing or drawing and calling people to him

with kindness, whether he is speaking of his relation to the
Father or to the world, can we discover the signs of inner
revolutions overcome, or the scars of any terrible conflict. Everything seems to pour from him naturally, as though it could not
do otherwise, like a spring from the depths of the earth, clear
and unchecked in its flow. Where shall we find the man who at
the age of thirty can so speak, if he has gone through bitter
struggles—struggles of the soul, in which he has ended by burning what he once adored, and by adoring what he burned?
Where shall we find the man who has broken with his past, in
order to summon others to repentance as well as himself, but
who through it all never speaks of his own repentance? This
consideration makes it impossible that his life could have been
spent in inner conflict, however little it may have been lacking
in deep emotion, in temptation, and in doubt.

One final point. The picture of Jesus' life and his discourses
stand in no relation with the Greek spirit. That is almost a
matter for surprise; for Galilee was full of Greeks, and Greek
was then spoken in many of its cities, much as Swedish is nowadays in Finland. There were Greek teachers and philosophers
there, and it is scarcely conceivable that Jesus should have been
entirely unacquainted with their language. But that he was in
any way influenced by them, that he was ever in touch with the
thoughts of Plato or the Porch, even though it may have been
only in some popular redaction, it is absolutely impossible to
maintain. Of course if religious individualism—God and the
soul, the soul and its God; if subjectivism; if the full self-
responsibility of the individual; if the separation of the religious
from the political—if all this is only Greek, then Jesus, too,
stands within the sphere of Greek development; then he, too,
breathed the pure air of Greece and drank from the Greek
spring. But it cannot be proved that it is only on this one line,
only in the Hellenic people, that this development took place;
nay, it is rather the contrary that can be shown; other nations
also advanced to similar states of knowledge and feeling;
although they mostly did so, it is true, only after Alexander the
Great had pulled down the barriers and fences which kept them
apart. For these nations, too, no doubt it was in the majority of

cases the Greek element that was the liberating and progressive factor. But I do not believe that the Psalmist who uttered the words, "Whom have I in heaven but thee? and there is none upon earth that I desire beside thee," had ever heard anything of Socrates or of Plato.

Enough : from their silence on the first thirty years of Jesus' life, and from what the evangelists do *not* tell us of the period of his activity, there are important things to be learnt.

He lived in religion, and it was breath to him in the fear of God; his whole life, all his thoughts and feelings, were absorbed in the relation to God; and yet he did not talk like an enthusiast and a fanatic, who sees only one red-hot spot, and so is blind to the world and all that it contains. He spoke his message and looked at the world with a fresh and clear eye for the life, great and small, that surrounded him. He proclaimed that to gain the whole world was nothing if the soul were injured, and yet he remained kind and sympathetic to every living thing. That is the most astonishing and the greatest fact about him! His discourses, generally clothed in parables and sayings, exhibit every degree of human speech and the whole range of the emotions. The sternest tones of passionate accusation and indignant reproof, nay, even irony, he does not despise; but they must have formed the exception with him. He is possessed of a quiet, uniform, collected demeanour, with everything directed to one goal. He never uses any ecstatic language, and the tone of stirring prophecy is rare. Entrusted with the greatest of all missions, his eye and ear are open to every impression of the life around him—a proof of intense calm and absolute certainty. "Mourning and weeping, laughing and dancing, wealth and poverty, hunger and thirst, health and sickness, children's play and politics, gathering and scattering, the leaving of home, life in the inn and the return, marriage and funeral, the splendid house of the living and the grave of the dead, the sower and the reaper in the field, the lord of the vintage among his vines, the idle workman in the market place, the shepherd searching for the sheep, the dealer in pearls on the sea, and, then again, the woman at home anxious over the barrel of meal and the leaven, or the lost piece of money, the widow's complaint to the surly official, the earthly food that perishes, the mental relation of teacher and pupil, on the one side regal glory and the tyrant's lust of power, on the other childish innocence and the industry of the servant —all these pictures enliven his discourse and make it clear even to those who are children in mind." They do more than tell us that he spoke in picture and parable. They exhibit an inner freedom and a cheerfulness of soul in the midst of the greatest strain, such as no prophet ever possessed before him. His eye rests kindly upon the flowers and the children, on the lily of the field—"Solomon in all his glory is not clothed like one of them" —on the birds in the air and the sparrows on the housetop. The sphere in which he lived, above the earth and its concerns, did not destroy his interest in it; no! he brought everything in it into relation with the God whom he knew, and he saw it as protected and preserved in Him: "Your Father in heaven feeds them." The parable is his most familiar form of speech. Insensibly, however, parable and sympathy with human lot pass into each other. Yet he who had not where to lay his head does not speak like one who has broken with everything, or like a heroic penitent, or like an ecstatic prophet, but like a man who has rest and peace for his soul, and is able to give life and strength to others. He strikes the mightiest notes; he offers men an inexorable alternative; he leaves them no escape : and yet the strongest emotion seems to come naturally to him, and he expresses it as something natural; he clothes it in the language in which a mother speaks to her child.

LECTURE THREE

In the previous lecture we spoke of our evangelists and of their silence on the subject of Jesus' early development. We described in brief the mode and character of his teaching. We saw that he spoke like a prophet and yet not like a prophet. His words breathe peace, joy, and certainty. He urges the necessity of struggle and decision—"where your treasure is, there will your heart be also"—and yet the equable calm of the parable is over all that he says : under God's sun and the dew of heaven everything is to grow and increase until the harvest. He lived in the continual consciousness of God's presence. His food and drink was to do God's will. But—and this seemed to us the greatest thing about him and the seal of his inner freedom—he did not speak like a heroic penitent, or like an ascetic who has turned his back upon the world. His eye rested kindly upon the whole world, and he saw it as it was, in all its varied and changing colours. He ennobled it in his parables; his gaze penetrated the veil of the earthly, and he recognised everywhere the hand of the living God.

When he came forward, another was already at work among the Jewish people : John the Baptist. Within a few months a great movement had arisen on the banks of the Jordan. It differed altogether from those Messianic movements which for several generations had by fits and starts kept the nation alive. The Baptist, it is true, also proclaimed that the kingdom of God was at hand; and what he meant was nothing less than the day of the Lord, the judgment, the end now coming. But the day of judgment which John the Baptist announced was not the great day when God was going to take vengeance upon the heathen and raise up his own people; it was the day of judgment for this very people that he prophesied. "Who hath warned you to flee from the wrath to come? Think not to say within yourselves, We have Abraham to our father : for I say unto you that God is able of these stones to raise up children unto Abraham. And now also the axe is laid unto the root of the trees." In that day of judgment it is not being children of Abraham, but doing works of righteousness, which is to turn the scale. And he, the preacher, himself began with repentance and devoted his life to it. He stands before them in raiment of camel's hair, and his meat is locusts and wild honey. But it is not in the levying of a band of ascetics that he sees his work, or at any rate his main work. He appeals to the whole nation, busy with its various trades and callings, and summons it to repentance. They seem very simple truths that he utters. To the publicans he says : "Exact no more than that which is appointed you"; to the soldiers : "Do violence to no man, neither accuse any falsely, and be content with your wages"; to the well-to-do : "He that hath two coats, let him impart to him that hath none, and he that hath meat, let him do likewise"; and to all : "Forget not the poor." This is the practical proof of the repentance to which he calls, and it embraces the conversion which he has in view. It is not a question of a single act, the baptism of repentance, but of a righteous life in the face of the avenging justice of God. Of ceremonies, sacrifices, and the works of the law, John did not speak; apparently he thought them unimportant. It was on a right disposition and good deeds that everything turned. In the day of judgment it was by this standard that the God of Abraham would judge.

Let us pause here for a moment. Questions force themselves upon us at this point which have often been answered and still are again and again put. It is clear that John the Baptist proclaimed the sovereignty of God and His holy moral law. It is also clear that he proclaimed to his fellow-countrymen that it was by the moral law that they were to measure, and that on this alone everything was to turn. He told them that what they were to care about most was to be in a right state within and to do good deeds. It is clear, lastly, there is nothing over-refined or artificial in his notion of what was good; he means ordinary morality. It is here that the questions arise.

Firstly : If it was only so simple a matter as the eternal claims of what is right and holy, why all this apparatus about the coming of the day of judgment, about the axe being laid to the root of the trees, about the unquenchable fire, and so on?

Secondly: Is not this baptism in the wilderness and this giving out that the day of judgment is at hand simply the reflection or the product of the political and social state of the nation at the time?

Thirdly: What is there that was really new in this message and had not already been expressed in Judaism?

These three questions are very intimately connected with one another.

Firstly, then, as to the whole dramatic eschatological apparatus about the coming of the kingdom of God, the end being at hand, and so on. Well, every time that a man earnestly, and out of the depths of his own personal experience, points others to God and to what is good and holy, whether it be deliverance or judgment that he preaches, it has always, so far as history tells us, taken the form of announcing that the end is at hand. How is that to be explained? The answer is not difficult. Not only is religion a life in and with God; but, just because it is that, it is also the revelation of the meaning and responsibility of life. Every one who has awakened to a sense of religion perceives that, without it, the search for such meaning is in vain, and that the individual, as well as the multitude, wanders aimlessly and falls: "they go astray, every one turns to his own way." But the prophet who has become conscious of God is filled with terror and agony as he recognises that all mankind is sunk in error and indifference. He feels like a traveller who sees his companions blindly rushing to the edge of a precipice. He wants to call them back at all costs. The time is running out; he can still warn them; he can still adjure them to turn back; in a single hour, perhaps, all will be lost. The time is running out, it is the last moment—this is the cry in which, then, in all nations and at all times, any energetic call to conversion has been voiced whenever a fresh prophet has been granted them. The prophet's gaze penetrates the course of history; he sees the irrevocable end; and he is filled with boundless astonishment that the godlessness and blindness, the frivolity and indolence, have not long since brought everything to utter ruin and destruction. That there is still a brief moment left in which conversion is possible seems to him the greatest marvel of all, and to be ascribed only to God's forbearance. But certain it is that the end cannot be very far off. This is the way in which with every great cry for repentance the idea of the approaching end always arises. The individual forms in which it shapes itself depend upon contemporary circumstances and are of subordinate importance. It is only the religion which has been built up into an intellectual system that does not make this emphasising of the end all-important; without such emphasis no actual religion is conceivable, whether it springs up anew like a sudden flame or glows in the soul like a secret fire.

I pass now to the second question : whether the social and political conditions of the time were not causes of the religious movement. Let us see briefly where we are. You are aware that at the time of which we speak the peaceful days of the Jewish theocracy were long past. For two centuries blow had followed upon blow; from the terrible days of Antiochus Epiphanes onwards the nation had never had any rest. The kingdom of the Maccabees had been set up, and through inner strife and external foe had soon disappeared again. The Romans had invaded the country and had laid their iron hand upon everything. The tyranny of that Edomite parvenu, King Herod, had robbed the nation of every pleasure in life and maimed it in all its members. So far as human foresight went, it looked as if no improvement in its position could ever again be effected; the lie seemed to be given to all the glorious old prophecies; the end appeared to have come. How easy it was at such an epoch to despair of all earthly things, and in this despair to renounce in utter distress what had once passed as the inseparable accompaniment of the theocracy. How easy it was now to declare the earthly crown, political possessions, prestige and wealth, strenuous effort and struggle, to be one and all worthless, and in place of them to look to heaven for a completely new kingdom, a kingdom for the poor, the oppressed, the weak, and to hope that their virtues of gentleness and patience would receive a crown. And if for hundreds of years the national God of Israel had been undergoing a transformation; if he had broken in pieces the weapons of the mighty, and derided the showy worship of his priests; if he had demanded righteous judgment and mercy—what a temptation there was to proclaim him as the God who wills to see his people in misery that he may then bring them deliverance! We can, in fact, with little trouble construct the religion and its hopes which seemed of necessity to result from the circumstances of the time—a miserabilism which clings to the expectation of a miraculous interference on God's part, and in the meantime, as it were, wallows in wretchedness.

But although the terrible circumstances of the time certainly disengaged and developed many ideas of this kind, and easily account for the wild enterprises of the false Messiahs and the political efforts of fanatical Pharisees, they are very far from being sufficient to explain John the Baptist's message. They do, indeed, explain how it was that deliverance from earthly things was an idea which seized hold of wide circles, and that people were looking to God. Trouble makes men pray. But trouble in itself does not give any moral force, and moral force was the chief element in John the Baptist's message. In appealing to it, in proclaiming that everything must be based on morality and personal responsibility, he took a higher point of view than the feeble piety of the "poor," and drew, not from time, but from eternity.

It is scarcely a century since Fichte delivered his memorable orations here in Berlin, after the terrible defeat which Germany had suffered. What did he do in these lectures? In the first place, he held up a mirror to the nation, and showed it its sins and their consequences—frivolity, godlessness, self-complacency, infatuation, weakness. What did he do next? Did he simply call them to arms? Arms were just what they were no longer capable of bearing; they had been struck from their powerless hands. It was to repentance and to inward conversion that he called them; to God, and therefore to the exertion of all their moral force; to truth and to the Spirit, so that by the Spirit everything might be made new. By his powerful personality, and in union with friends of a like mind, he produced an immense impression. He succeeded in opening up once more the choked fountains of our energy, because he knew the strength from which help comes and had drunk of the living water himself. No doubt the necessities of the time taught him and steeled him; but it would be foolish and ridiculous to maintain that Fichte's orations were the product of the general woe. They were the antithesis of it. Not otherwise must we think of John the Baptist's message, and—let me say it at once—of the message which Jesus himself delivered. That they appealed to those who expected nothing of the world or of politics (of John the Baptist, however, this is not directly reported); that they would have nothing to do with those popular leaders who led the people to ruin; that they turned their gaze altogether from earthly things, may also be accounted for by the circumstances of the time. But the remedy which they proclaimed was no product of those circumstances. Nay, to invoke only the ordinary canons of morality and expect everything of them—was it not bound to seem a hopeless enterprise? Whence came the power, the inflexible power, which compelled others? This leads us to the last of the questions which we have raised.

Thirdly, what was there that was new in the whole movement? Was it anything new to set up the sovereignty of God, the sovereignty of the good and the holy, in opposition to all the other elements which had forced their way into religion? Did John the Baptist, did Christ himself, come with any message that had not been proclaimed long before? Gentlemen, the question as to what is new in religion is not a question which is raised by those who live in it. What is there that can have been "new," seeing that mankind existed so long before Jesus Christ and had witnessed so much in the way of intelligence and knowledge? Monotheism had long been introduced, and the few possible types of monotheistic religious fervour had long made their appearance here and there, and had taken possession of whole schools, nay, of a whole nation. Can the religious individualism of that Psalmist ever be surpassed in depth and vigour who confessed: "Lord, when I have thee, I ask not after heaven and earth"? Can we go beyond what Micah said: "He hath showed thee, O man, what is good; and what doth the Lord require of thee but to do justly and to love mercy, and to walk humbly with thy God"? Centuries had elapsed since these words were spoken. "What do you want, then, with your Christ?" we are asked, chiefly by Jewish scholars; "he introduced nothing new." I answer with Wellhausen: It is quite true that what Jesus proclaimed, what John the Baptist expressed before him in his exhortations to repentance, was also to be found in the prophets, and even in the Jewish tradition of their time. The Pharisees themselves were in possession of it; but unfortunately they were in possession of much else besides. With them it was weighted, darkened, distorted, rendered ineffective and deprived of its force, by a thousand things which they also took to be a part of religion just as important as mercy and judgment. They reduced everything to one dead level, wove everything into one fabric; the good and holy was only one woof in a broad earthly warp. You ask again, then: "What was there that was new?" The question is out of place in monotheistic religion. Ask rather: "What was here proclaimed, had it any strength and was it pure?" I answer: Take the people of Israel and search the whole history of their religion, take history generally, and where will you find any message about God and the good that was ever so pure and so full of strength—for purity and strength go together—as we hear and read of in the Gospels? As regards purity, the spring of holiness had, indeed, long been opened; but it was choked with sand and dirt, and its water was polluted. The rabbis and theologians who came in afterwards and tried to distil this water, even if successfully, made no difference. Now, however, the spring burst forth afresh, and broke a new way for itself through the rubbish—through the rubbish which priests and theologians had heaped up so as to smother the true element in religion; for how often does it happen in history that theology is only the instrument for getting rid of religion! As for the other element, that of strength, Pharisaical teachers had proclaimed that everything was contained in the injunction to love God and neighbour. They spoke excellently; the words might have come out of Jesus' mouth. But what was the result of their language? That the nation, that in particular their own pupils, condemned the man who took the words seriously. All that they did was weak and, because weak, harmful. What produces the effect is not words; it is the power of the personality that stands behind them. "He taught as one having authority and not as the Scribes"—such was the impression of him which his disciples received. His words became to them "the words of life," seeds which sprang up and bore fruit. That was what was new.

Some such message John the Baptist had already begun to deliver. He, too, had undoubtedly placed himself in opposition to the leaders of the people; for any man who tells people to "reform," and at the same time enjoins nothing more than repentance and good works, always comes into opposition with the official leaders of religion and church. But beyond the lines of the message of repentance John did not go.

Jesus Christ then appeared. He first of all accepted and affirmed the Baptist's message to its full extent, and he acknowledged the Baptist himself; nay, there was no one of whom he spoke in language of such warm recognition. Did not he say that among them that were born of women there had not arisen a greater than John the Baptist? Again and again he acknowledged that his cause began with the Baptist and that the Baptist was his forerunner. Nay, he had had himself baptised by him, and had thereby put himself into the movement which the Baptist began.

But he did not rest there. When he appeared, he, too, it is true, like John proclaimed: "Repent, for the kingdom of God is at hand"; but his message became one of joy as he delivered it. The traditions about him contain nothing more certain than that his message was an "evangel," and that it was felt to bring blessing and joy. With good reason, therefore, the evangelist Luke began his narrative of Jesus' public appearance with the words of the prophet Isaiah: *"The Spirit of the Lord is upon me, because he hath anointed me to preach the Gospel to the poor; he hath sent me to heal the broken-hearted, to preach deliverance to the captives and recovering of sight to the blind, to set at liberty them that are bruised, to preach the acceptable year of the Lord."* Or in Jesus' own words: *"Come unto me, all ye that labour and are heavy laden, and I will give you rest. Take my yoke upon you, and learn of me; for I am meek and lowly of heart; and ye shall find rest unto your souls. For my yoke is easy and my burden is light."* These words dominated Jesus' whole work and message; they contain the theme of all that he taught and did. They make it at once obvious that in this teaching of his he left John the Baptist's message far behind. The latter, although already in silent conflict with the priests and the scribes, did not become a definite signal for contradiction. "The falling and the rising again," a new humanity opposed to the old, men of God—these Jesus Christ was the first to create. He came into immediate opposition with the official leaders of the people, and in them with ordinary human nature in general. They thought of God as of a despot guarding the ceremonial observances in His household; he breathed in the presence of God. They saw Him only in His law, which they had converted into a labyrinth of dark defiles, blind alleys and secret passages; he saw and felt Him everywhere. They were in possession of a thousand of His commandments, and thought, therefore, that they knew Him; he had one only, and that was why he knew Him. They had made this religion into an earthly trade, and there was nothing more detestable; he proclaimed the living God and the soul's nobility.

If, however, we take a general view of Jesus' teaching, we shall see that it may be grouped under three heads. They are each of such a nature as to contain the whole, and hence it can be exhibited in its entirety under any one of them.

Firstly, the kingdom of God and its coming.

Secondly, God the Father and the infinite value of the human soul.

Thirdly, the higher righteousness and the commandment of love.

That Jesus' message is so great and so powerful lies in the fact that it is so simple and on the other hand so rich; so simple as to be exhausted in each of the leading thoughts which he uttered; so rich that every one of these thoughts seems to be inexhaustible and the full meaning of the sayings and parables beyond our reach. But more than that—he himself stands behind everything that he said. His words speak to us across the centuries with the freshness of the present. It is here that that profound saying is truly verified "Speak, that I may see thee."

Our course in what follows will be to try to learn what those three heads are, and to classify the thoughts which come under them. They contain the main features of Jesus' message. We shall then try to understand the Gospel in its relations to certain great questions of life.

I. *The kingdom of God and its coming*

Jesus' message of the kingdom of God runs through all the forms and statements of the prophecy which, taking its colour from the Old Testament, announces the day of judgment and the visible government of God in the future, up to the idea of an inward coming of the kingdom, starting with Jesus' message and then beginning. His message embraces these two poles, with many stages between them that shade off one into another. At the one pole the coming of the kingdom seems to be a purely future event and the kingdom itself to be the eternal rule of God; at the other, it appears as something inward, something which is already present and making its entrance at the moment. You see, therefore, that neither the conception of the kingdom of God, nor the way in which its coming is represented, is free from ambiguity. Jesus took it from the religious traditions of his nation, where it already occupied a foremost place; he accepted various aspects of it in which the conception was still a living force, and he added new ones. Eudæmonistic expectations of a mundane and political character were all that he discarded.

Jesus, like all those of his own nation who were really in earnest, was profoundly conscious of the great antithesis between the kingdom of God and that kingdom of the world in which he saw the reign of evil and the evil one. This was no mere image or empty idea; it was a truth which he saw and felt most vividly. He was certain, then, that the kingdom of the world must perish and be destroyed. But nothing short of a battle can effect it. With dramatic intensity battle and victory stand like a picture before his soul, drawn in those large firm lines in which the prophets had seen them. At the close of the drama he sees himself seated at the right hand of his Father, and his twelve

disciples on thrones judging the twelve tribes of Israel; so objective was this picture to him, so completely in harmony with the
ideas of his time. Now we may take the view—and not a few
of us take it—that in these dramatic pictures, with their hard
colours and contrasts, we have the actual purport of Jesus' message and the fundamental form which it took; and that all his
other statements of it must be simply regarded as secondary. We
may say that they are all variations of it more or less edifying,
variations which were added, perhaps, only by later reporters;
but that the only positive factor is the dramatic hope for the
future. In this view I cannot concur. It is considered a perverse
proceeding in similar cases to judge eminent, epoch-making personalities first and foremost by what they share with their contemporaries, and on the other hand to put everything great and
characteristic in them into the background. The tendency to
reduce everything as far as possible to one level, and to efface
what is special and individual, may spring in some minds from
a praiseworthy sense of truth, but it has proved misleading.
More frequently, however, we get the endeavour, conscious or
unconscious, to refuse greatness any recognition at all, and to
throw down anything that is exalted. There can be no doubt
about the fact that the idea of the two kingdoms, of God and of
the devil, and their conflicts, and of that last conflict at some
future time when the devil, long cast out of heaven, will be also
defeated on earth, was an idea which Jesus simply shared with
his contemporaries. He did not start it, but he grew up in it and
he retained it. The other view, however, that the kingdom of
God "cometh not with observation," that it is already here, was
his own.

For us, gentlemen, to-day, it is difficult to reconcile, nay, it is
scarcely possible to bridge over, such an opposition as is involved,
on the one side in a dramatic picture of God's kingdom existing
in the future, and on the other in the announcement that "it is
in the midst of you," a still and mighty power in the hearts of
men. But to understand why it was that with other historical
traditions and other forms of culture no opposition was felt to
exist between these views, nay, that both were able to exist side
by side, we must reflect, we must steep ourselves in the history

of the past. I imagine that a few hundred years hence people will also discover in the intellectual ideas which we shall have left behind us much that is contradictory, and they will wonder how we put up with it. They will find much hard and dry husk in what we took for kernel; they will be unable to understand how we could be so short-sighted, or have failed to get a sound grasp of what was essential and separate it from the rest. Some day the knife will be applied and pieces will be cut away where as yet we do not feel the slightest inclination to distinguish. Let us hope that we may then find fair judges, who will measure our ideas, not by what we have unwittingly taken over from tradition and are neither able nor called upon to correct, but by what was born of our very own, by the changes and improvements which we have effected in what was handed down to us or was commonly prevalent in our day.

Truly the historian's task of distinguishing between what is traditional and what is peculiar, between kernel and husk, in Jesus' message of the kingdom of God, is a difficult and responsible one. How far may we go? We surely cannot want to rob this message of its innate quality and colour; we cannot want to change it into a pale scheme of ethics. On the other hand, we cannot want to lose sight of its peculiar character and strength, as we should do were we to side with those who resolve it into the general ideas prevailing at the time. The very way in which Jesus distinguished between the traditional elements—he left out none in which there was a spark of moral force, and he accepted none which encouraged the selfish expectations of his nation—this very discrimination teaches us that it was from a deeper knowledge that he spoke and taught. But we possess testimonies of a much more striking kind. If anyone wants to know what the kingdom of God and the coming of it meant in Jesus' message, he must read and study his parables. He will then see what it is that is meant. The kingdom of God comes by coming to the individual, by entering into his soul and laying hold of it. True, the kingdom of God is the rule of God; but it is the rule of the holy God in the hearts of individuals; *it is God Himself in His power*. From this point of view everything that was dramatic in the external and historical sense has vanished;

and gone, too, are all the external hopes for the future. Take whatever parable you will, the parable of the sower, of the pearl of great price, of the treasure buried in the field—the word of God, God Himself, is the kingdom. It is not a question of angels and devils, thrones and principalities, but of God and the soul, the soul and its God.

LECTURE FOUR

WE LAST spoke of Jesus' message in so far as it proclaimed the kingdom of God and its coming. We saw that it runs through all the forms in which the prophecy of the day of judgment is expressed in the Old Testament, up to the idea of an inward coming of the kingdom then beginning. Finally we tried to show why the latter idea is to be regarded as the dominant one. Before examining it more closely, however, I should like to draw your attention to two particularly important expressions of it, lying between the extremes of the "day of judgment" and the "inner coming."

In the first of them, the coming of God's kingdom means the destruction of the devil's, and victory over the demons. Hitherto it is they who have been ruling; having taken possession of men and even of whole nations, they are forcing them to their will. Jesus not only declares that he is come to destroy the works of the devil, but he actually drives out the demons and releases men from their power.

Let me here digress a little from our subject. Nothing in the Gospels strikes us as stranger than the frequently recurring stories of demons, and the great importance which the evangelists attach to them. For many among us the very fact that these writings report such absurdities is sufficient reason for declining to accept them. Now in this connexion it is well to know that absolutely similar stories are to be found in numerous writings of that age, Greek, Roman, and Jewish. The notion of people being "possessed" was current everywhere; nay, even the science of the time looked upon a whole section of morbid phenomena in this light. But the consequence of these phenomena being explained as meaning that some evil and invisible power had taken possession of a man, was that mental afflictions took forms which looked as if an alien being had really entered into the soul. There is nothing paradoxical in this. If modern science were to declare nervous disease to consist, in great part, of "possession," and the newspapers were to spread this announcement amongst the public, the same thing would recur. We should soon have numerous cases in which nervous patients looked as if they were in the grip of an evil spirit, and themselves believed that they were so. Theory and belief would work by suggestion and again create a class of "demoniacs" amongst the insane, just as they created them hundreds, nay thousands of years ago. It is unhistorical and foolish to attribute any peculiar notion or "theory" about demons and the demoniac to the Gospels and the evangelists. They only shared the general notions of their time. The forms of mental disease in question are of rare occurrence nowadays, but nevertheless they are not yet quite extinct. Where they occur the best means of encountering them is to-day, as it was formerly, the influence of a strong personality. It is able to threaten and subdue the "devil," and so heal the patient. In Palestine "demoniacs" must have been particularly numerous. Jesus saw in them the forces of evil and mischief, and by his marvellous power over the souls of those who trusted him he banished the disease. This brings us to the second point.

When John the Baptist in prison was disturbed by doubts as to whether Jesus was "he who was to come," he sent two of his own disciples to him to ask him himself. There is nothing more touching than this question of the Baptist's, nothing more edifying than the Lord's answer. But let us not dwell upon the scene itself. What was the answer? "Go and shew John again those things which you do hear and see : the blind receive their sight, and the lame walk, the lepers are cleansed, and the deaf hear, the dead are raised up, and the poor have the Gospel preached to them." That is what the "coming of the kingdom" means, or, rather, it is there already in this saving activity. By vanquishing and banishing misery, need and disease, by the actual influence which Jesus was exerting, John was to see that a new day had dawned. The healing of the possessed was only a part of this saving activity; *the activity itself, however, was what Jesus denoted as the meaning and the seal of his mission.*

It was, then, to the wretched, to the sick, and to the poor, that he addressed himself; but not as a moralist and without any trace of weak-minded sentimentality. He makes no division of evils into departments and groups; he spends no time in asking whether the sick one "deserves" to be healed; he is far, too, from being sympathetical about pain and death. He nowhere says that disease is salutary and that evil is a blessing. No! disease he calls disease, and health he calls health. To him all evil, all misery, is something terrible; it is part of the great realm of Satan; yet he feels the power of the Saviour within him, and he knows that progress is possible only by overcoming weakness and healing disease.

But this is not all. It is by his healing, above all by his forgiving sin, that the kingdom of God comes. Here we have the first complete transition to the conception of the kingdom of God as the power that works inwardly. As he calls the sick and the poor to him, so he calls sinners also, and it is this call which is all-important. "The Son of Man is come to seek and to save that which was lost." Here for the first time everything that is external and merely future is abandoned: it is the individual, not the nation or the state, which is redeemed; it is *new men* who are to arise, and the kingdom of God is to be at once their strength and the goal at which they aim. They search for the treasure hidden in the field and find it; they sell all that they have and buy the pearl of great price; they are converted and become as children; but thereby they are redeemed and made God's children and God's champions.

It was in this connexion that Jesus spoke of the kingdom of God which the violent take by force; and, again, of the kingdom of God which grows steadily and silently like a seed and bears fruit. It is in its very nature a spiritual force, a power which sinks into a man within, and can be understood only from within. Thus, although the kingdom is also in heaven; although it will come with the day of judgment, he can still say of it; "It is not here or there, it is within you."

At a later period the view of the kingdom, according to which it was already come and still comes in Jesus' saving activity, was not kept up by his disciples: nay, they continued to speak of it as of something that was solely in the future. But the thing itself retained its force; it was only given another title. It underwent the same experience as the conception of the "Messiah." As we shall see hereafter, there was scarcely anyone in the Church of the Gentiles who sought to explain Jesus' significance by regarding him as the "Messiah." But the thing itself did not perish.

The essential elements in the message of the kingdom were preserved. The kingdom has a triple meaning. Firstly, it is something supernatural, a gift from above, not a product of ordinary life. Secondly, it is a purely religious blessing, the inner link with the living God; thirdly, it is the most important experience that a man can have, that on which everything else depends; it permeates and dominates his whole existence, because sin is forgiven and misery banished.

Without this kingdom, which comes to the humble and makes them new men and joyful, the meaning and the aim of life would not be laid bare. This was what Jesus himself found, and what his disciples found. It is by the supernatural element alone that we can ever get at the meaning of life; for natural existence ends in death, and a life that is bound up with death can have no meaning. This is a fact to which only sophisms can blind us. Here, however, the kingdom of God, the Eternal, entered into time. "Eternal light came in and made the world look new." This is Jesus' message of the kingdom. Everything else that he proclaimed can be brought into connexion with this; his whole "doctrine" can be conceived as a message of the kingdom. But we shall recognise this, and the blessing which he means, still more clearly, if we turn to the second of the sections indicated in the previous lecture, and thereby progressively acquaint ourselves with the fundamental features of Jesus' message.

II. *God the Father and the infinite value of the human soul*

To our modern way of thinking and feeling, Christ's message appears in the clearest and most direct light when grasped in connexion with the idea of God the Father and the infinite value of the human soul. Here the elements which I would describe as the restful and rest-giving in Jesus' message, and which are comprehended in the idea of our being children of God, find expression. I call them *restful* in contrast with the impulsive and stirring elements; although it is just they that are informed with a special strength. But the fact that the whole of Jesus' message may be reduced to these two heads—God as the Father, and the human soul so ennobled that it can and does unite with Him—shows us that the Gospel is in no wise a positive religion like the rest; that it contains no statutory or particularistic elements; *that it is, therefore, religion itself.* It is superior to all antithesis and tension between this world and a world to come, between reason and ecstasy, between work in the world and holding aloof from it, between Judaism and Hellenism. It can dominate them all, and to no sphere of earthly life is it confined or necessarily tied down. Let us, however, get a clearer idea of what being children of God, in Jesus' sense, means, by briefly considering four groups of sayings, or, as the case may be, single sayings of his, viz.: (1) The Lord's Prayer; (2) that utterance, "Rejoice not that the spirits are subject unto you; but rather rejoice because your names are written in heaven"; (3) the words "Are not two sparrows sold for a farthing? and one of them shall not fall on the ground without your Father. But the very hairs of your head are all numbered"; and lastly (4), "What shall it profit a man if he shall gain the whole world and lose his own soul?"

Let us take the Lord's Prayer first. It was communicated by Jesus to his disciples at a particularly solemn moment. They had asked him to teach them how to pray, as John the Baptist had taught his disciples. Thereupon he uttered the Lord's Prayer. It is by their prayers that the character of all higher religions is determined. This prayer, however, is spoken—as every one must feel who has ever given it a thought in his soul—by one who has overcome all inner unrest, or overcomes it the moment that he goes before God. The very apostrophe of the prayer, "Our Father," exhibits the steady faith of the man who knows that he is safe in God, and it tells us that he is certain of being heard. Not to hurl violent desires at heaven or to obtain this or

that earthly blessing does he pray, but to preserve the power
which he already possesses and strengthen the union with God
in which he lives. No one, then, can utter this prayer unless
his heart is in profound peace and his mind wholly concentrated
on the inner relation of the soul with God. All other prayers
are of a lower order, for they go into particulars or are so
framed that in some way or other they stir the imagination in
regard to the things of sense as well; whilst this prayer leads us
away from everything to the height where the soul is alone with
its God. And yet the earthly element is not absent. The whole
of the second half of the prayer deals with earthly relations,
but they are placed in the light of the Eternal. In vain will you
look for any request for particular gifts of grace, or special
blessings, even of a spiritual kind. "All else shall be added unto
you." The name of God, His will, and His kingdom—these
elements of rest and permanence are diffused over the earthly
relations as well. Everything that is small and selfish melts away,
and only four things are left with regard to which it is worth
while to pray—the daily bread, the daily trespass, the daily
temptations, and the evil in life. There is nothing in the Gospels
that tells us more certainly what the Gospel is, and what sort
of disposition and temper it produces, than the Lord's Prayer.
With this prayer all those who disparage the Gospel by representing it as an ascetic or ecstatic or sociological pronouncement
ought to be confronted. It shows the Gospel to be the Fatherhood of God applied to the whole of life; to be an inner union
with God's will and God's kingdom, and a joyous certainty of
the possession of eternal blessings and protection from evil.

As to the second utterance: when Jesus says "Rejoice not
that the spirits are subject unto you, but rejoice rather that
your names are written in heaven," it is another way of laying
special emphasis on the idea that the all-important element in
this religion is the consciousness of being safe in God. The
greatest achievements, nay, the very works which are done in
the strength of this religion, fall below the assurance, at once
humble and proud, of resting for time and eternity under the
fatherly care of God. Moreover, the genuineness, nay, the actual

existence, of religious experience is to be measured, not by any transcendency of feeling or by great deeds that all men can see, but by the joy and the peace which are diffused through the soul that can say "My Father."

How far did Christ carry this idea of the fatherly providence of God? Here we come to the third saying: "Are not two sparrows sold for a farthing; and one of them shall not fall to the ground without your Father. But the very hairs of your head are all numbered." The assurance that God rules is to go as far as our fears go, nay, as far as life itself—life down even to its smallest manifestations in the order of Nature. It was to disabuse his disciples of the fear of evil and the terrors of death that he gave them the sayings about the sparrows and the flowers of the field; they are to learn how to see the hand of the living God everywhere in life, and in death too.

Finally, in asking—and after what has gone before the question can hardly surprise us—"What shall it profit a man if he shall gain the whole world and lose his own soul?" he put a man's value as high as it can be put. The man who can say "My Father" to the Being who rules heaven and earth is thereby raised above heaven and earth, and himself has a value which is higher than all the fabric of this world. But this great saying took the stern tone of a warning. He offered them a gift and with it set them a task. How different was the Greek doctrine! Plato, it is true, had already sung the great hymn of the mind; he had distinguished it from the whole world of appearance and maintained its eternal origin. But the mind which he meant was the knowing mind; he contrasted it with blind, insensible matter; his message made its appeal to the wise. Jesus Christ calls to every poor soul: he calls to every one who bears a human face: You are children of the living God, and not only better than many sparrows but of more value than the whole world. The value of a truly great man, as I saw it put lately, consists in his increasing the value of all mankind. There is, indeed, nothing more significant in great men than this, that they have enhanced, that is, have progressively given effect to, human value, to the value of that race of men which has risen up out of the dull ground of Nature. But Jesus Christ was the first to bring the value of every human soul to light, and what he did no one can any more undo. We may take up what relation to him we will; in the history of the past no one can refuse to recognise that it was he who raised humanity to this level.

This highest estimate of a man's value is based on a transvaluation of all values. To the man who boasts of his possessions he says : "Thou fool." He confronts every one with the thought : "Whosoever will lose his life shall save it." He can even say : "He that hateth his life in this world shall keep it unto life eternal." This is the transvaluation of values of which many before him had a dim idea; of which they perceived the truth as through a veil; the redeeming power of which—that blessed mystery—they felt in advance. He was the first to give it calm, simple, and fearless expression, as though it were a truth which grew on every tree. It was just this that stamped his peculiar genius, that he gave perfectly simple expression to profound and all-important truths, as though they could not be otherwise; as though he were uttering something that was self-evident; as though he were only reminding men of what they all know already, because it lives in the innermost part of their souls.

In the combination of these ideas—God the Father, Providence, the position of men as God's children, the infinite value of the human soul—the whole Gospel is expressed. But we must recognise what a paradox it all is; nay, that the paradox of religion here for the first time finds its full expression. Measured by the experience of the senses and by exact knowledge, not only are the different religions a paradox, but so are all religious phenomena. They introduce an element, and pronounce it to be the most important of all, which is not cognisable by the senses, and flies in the face of things as they are actually constituted. All religions, however, other than Christianity are in some way so bound up with the things of the world that they involve an element of earthly advantage, or, as the case may be, are akin in their substance to the intellectual and spiritual condition of a definite epoch. But what can be less obvious than the statement: the hairs of your head are all numbered; you have a supernatural value; you can put yourselves into the hands of a power which no one has seen? Either that is nonsense, or else it is the utmost development of which religion is capable; no longer a mere phenomenon accompanying the life of the senses, a co-efficient, a transfiguration of certain parts of that life, but something which sets up a paramount title to be the first and the only fact that reveals the fundamental basis and meaning of life. Religion subordinates to itself the whole motley world of phenomena, and defies that world if it claims to be the only real one. Religion offers us only a single experience, but one which presents the world in a new light: the Eternal appears; time becomes means to an end; man is in his place on the side of the Eternal. This was certainly Jesus' meaning, and to take anything from it is to destroy it. In applying the idea of Providence to the whole of humanity and the world without any exception; in showing that humanity is rooted in the Eternal; in proclaiming the fact that we are God's children as at once a gift and a task, he took a vigorous hold of all fumbling and stammering attempts at religion and brought them to their issue. Once more let it be said: we may assume what position we will in regard to him and his message, certain it is that thence onward the value of our race is enhanced; human lives, nay, we ourselves, have become dearer to one another. A man may know it or not, but a real reverence for humanity follows from the practical recognition of God as the Father of us all.

III. *The higher righteousness and the commandment of love*

This is the third head, and the whole of the Gospel is embraced under it. To represent the Gospel as an ethical message is no depreciation of its value. The ethical system which Jesus found prevailing in his nation was both ample and profound. To judge the moral ideas of the Pharisees solely by their childish and casuistical aspects is wrong. By being bound up with religious worship and petrified in ritual observance, the morality of holiness had, indeed, been transformed into something that was the clear opposite of it. But all was not yet hard and dead; there was some life still left in the deeper parts of the system. To those who questioned him Jesus could still answer: "You have the law, keep it; you know best yourselves what you have to do; the sum of the law is, as you yourselves say, to love God and your neighbour." Nevertheless, there is a sphere of ethical thought which is peculiarly expressive of Jesus' Gospel. Let us make this clear by citing four points.

Firstly: Jesus severed the connexion existing in his day between ethics and external forms of religious worship and technical observance. He would have absolutely nothing to do with the purposeful and self-seeking pursuit of "good works" in combination with the ritual of worship. He exhibited an indignant contempt for men who allow their neighbours, nay, even their parents, to starve, and on the other hand send gifts to the temple. He will have no compromise in the matter. Love and mercy are ends in themselves; they lose all value and are put to shame by having to be anything else than the service of one's neighbour.

Secondly: in all questions of morality he goes straight to the root, that is, to the disposition and the intention. It is only thus that what he calls the "higher righteousness" can be understood. The "higher righteousness" is the righteousness that will stand when the depths of the heart are probed. Here, again, we have something that is seemingly very simple and self-evident. Yet the truth, as he uttered it, took the severe form: "It was said of old . . . but I say unto you." After all, then, the truth was something new; he was aware that it had never yet been expressed in such a consistent form and with such claims to supremacy. A large portion of the so-called Sermon on the Mount is occupied with what he says when he goes in detail through the several departments of human relationships and human failings so as to bring the disposition and intention to light in each case, to judge a man's works by them, and make heaven and hell depend on them.

Thirdly: what he freed from its connexion with self-seeking

and ritual elements, and recognised as the moral principle, he reduces to *one* root and to *one* motive—love. He knows of no other, and love itself, whether it takes the form of love of one's neighbour or of one's enemy, or the love of the Samaritan, is of one kind only. It must completely fill the soul; it is what remains when the soul dies to itself. In this sense love is the new life already begun. But it is always the love which *serves*, and only in this function does it exist and live.

Fourthly: we saw that Jesus freed the moral element from all alien connexions, even from its alliance with the public religion. When people say that the Gospel is a matter of ordinary morality, this is not to misunderstand him. And yet there is one all-important point where he combines religion and morality. It is a point which must be felt; it is not easy to define. In view of the Beatitudes it may, perhaps, best be described as *humility*. Jesus made love and humility one. Humility is not a virtue by itself; it is a purely receptive attitude, the expression of inner need, the prayer for God's grace and forgiveness; in a word, the opening up of the heart to God. In Jesus' view, this humility, which is the love of God of which we are capable—take, for instance, the parable of the Pharisee and the Publican—is an abiding disposition towards the good; it is that out of which everything that is good springs and grows. "Forgive us our trespasses even as we forgive them that trespass against us" is the prayer at once of humility and of love. This, then, is the source and origin of the love of one's neighbour; the poor in spirit and those who hunger and thirst after righteousness are also the peacemakers and the merciful.

It was in this sense that Jesus combined religion and morality, and in this sense religion may be called the soul of morality, and morality the body of religion. We can thus understand how it was that Jesus could place the love of God and the love of one's neighbour side by side; the love of one's neighbour is the only practical proof on earth of that love of God which finds its life in humility.

In thus expressing his message of the higher righteousness and the new commandment of love in these four leading thoughts, Jesus defined the sphere of the ethical in a way in which no one before him had ever defined it. But if ever we are threatened with doubts as to what he meant, we must steep ourselves again and again in the Beatitudes of the Sermon on the Mount. They contain his ethics and his religion, united at the root, and freed from all external and particularistic elements.

LECTURE FIVE

AT THE close of the last lecture I referred to the Beatitudes, and mentioned that they exhibit Jesus' religion in a particularly impressive way. I desire to remind you of another passage which shows that Jesus recognised the practical proof of religion to consist in the exercise of neighbourly love and mercy. In one of his last discourses he spoke of the Judgment, bringing it before his hearers' eyes in the parable of the shepherd separating the sheep from the goats. The sole principle of separation is the question of mercy. The question is raised by asking whether men gave food and drink to Jesus himself, and visited him; that is to say, it is put as a *religious* question. The paradox is then resolved in the sentence: "Inasmuch as ye have done it unto one of the least of these my brethren, ye have done it unto me." We can have no clearer illustration of the fact that in Jesus' view mercy was the quality on which everything turned, and that the temper in which it is exercised is the guarantee that a man's *religious* position is the right one. How so? Because in exercising this virtue men are imitating God: "Be merciful, even as your Father in heaven is merciful." He who exercises mercy exercises God's prerogative; for God's justice is not accomplished by keeping to the rule "an eye for an eye and a tooth for a tooth," but is subject to the power of His mercy.

Let us pause here for a moment. The history of religion marked an enormous advance, religion itself was established afresh, when through poets and thinkers in Greece on the one hand, and through the prophets in Palestine on the other, the idea of righteousness and a righteous God became a living force and transformed tradition. The gods were raised to a higher level and civilised; the warlike and capricious Jehovah became a holy Being in whose court of judgment a man might trust, albeit in fear and trembling. The two great provinces of religion and morality, hitherto separated, were now brought into close relation; for "the God-head is holy and just." It is *our* history that was then developed; for without that all-important transformation there would be no such thing as "mankind," no such thing as a "history of the world" in the higher sense. The most immediate result of this development may be summed up in the maxim: "What ye would not that men should do unto you, do ye also not unto them." Insufficient and prosaic as the rule may seem, yet, if extended so as to cover all human relationships and really observed, it contains a civilising force of enormous strength.

But it does not contain the ultimate step. Not until justice was compelled to give way to mercy, and the idea of brotherhood and self-sacrifice in the service of one's neighbour became paramount, was the last advance accomplished that it was possible and necessary to make. Here, again, religion received a fresh foundation. Its maxim, "What ye would that men should do unto you, do ye also unto them," may also seem prosaic; and yet rightly understood it leads to the summit and comprises a new method of apprehension, and a new way of judging one's own life. The thought that "he who loses his life he shall save it," runs side by side with this maxim and effects a transvaluation of values in the certainty that a man's true life is not tied to this span of time and is not rooted in material existence.

I hope that I have thus shown, however briefly, that in the sphere of thought which is indicated by "the higher righteousness" and "the new commandment of love" Jesus' teaching is also contained in its entirety. As a matter of fact, the three spheres which we have distinguished—the kingdom of God, God as the Father and the infinite value of the human soul, and the higher righteousness showing itself in love—coalesce; for ultimately the kingdom is nothing but the treasure which the soul possesses in the eternal and merciful God. Taking Jesus' sayings as its groundwork, it needs only a very little trouble to develop this thought into everything that Christendom has known and strives to maintain as hope, faith, and love.

To proceed; Now that we have established the fundamental characteristics of Jesus' message, let us try, in the second place, to treat of the main bearings of the Gospel as applied to individual problems. There are six points or questions which call for special attention, as being the most important in themselves, and consequently felt and regarded as such in all ages. And although, in the course of the Church's history, one or other of these questions may have passed into the background for a decade or two, it has always reappeared afresh, and with redoubled force :

(1) The Gospel and the world, or the question of asceticism;

(2) The Gospel and the poor, or the social question;

(3) The Gospel and the law, or the question of public order;

(4) The Gospel and work, or the question of civilisation;

(5) The Gospel and the Son of God, or the Christological question;

(6) The Gospel and doctrine, or the question of creed.

By these six questions—the first four hang together, and the last two stand by themselves—I hope to be able to exhibit, of course only in outline, the most important bearings of Jesus' message.

(1) *The Gospel and the world, or the question of asceticism*

There is a widespread opinion—it is dominant in the Catholic Churches, and many Protestants share it nowadays—that, in the last resort and in the most important things which it enjoins, the Gospel is a strictly world-shunning and ascetic creed. Some people proclaim this piece of intelligence with sympathy and admiration; nay, they magnify it into the contention that the whole value and meaning of genuine Christianity, as of Buddhism, lies in its world-denying character. Others emphasise the world-shunning doctrines of the Gospel in order thereby to expose its incompatibility with modern ethical principles, and to prove its uselessness as a religion. The Catholic Churches have found a curious way out of the difficulty, and one which is, in reality, a product of despair. They recognise, as I have said, the world-denying character of the Gospel, and they teach, accordingly, that it is only in the form of monasticism—that is, in the "vita religiosa"—that true Christian life finds its expression. But they admit a "lower" kind of Christianity without asceticism, as "sufficient." We will say nothing about this strange concession now; the Catholic doctrine is that it is only monks who can follow Christ fully. With this doctrine a great philosopher, and a still greater writer, of the nineteenth century, has made common cause. Schopenhauer extols Christianity because, and in so far as, it has produced great ascetics like St. Anthony or St. Francis; but, beyond that, everything in the Christian message seems to him to be useless and a stumbling-block. With a much deeper insight than a Schopenhauer, and with a strength of feeling and power of language that carry us away, Tolstoi has emphasised the ascetic and world-shunning features of the Gospel, and erected them into a rule of observance. That the ascetic ideal which he derives from the Gospel is endowed with warmth and strength, and includes the service of one's neighbour, is a fact which we cannot deny; but to him, too, the shunning of the world is the leading characteristic of Christianity. There are thousands of our "educated" readers who find his stories suggestive and exciting, but who at the bottom of their hearts are pleased and relieved to know that Christianity means the denial of the world; for then they know very well that it does not concern them. They are certain, and rightly certain, that this world is given them to be made the best of, within the bounds of its own blessings and its own regulations; and that if Christianity makes any other claim, it thereby shows that it is unnatural. If Christianity has no goal to set before this life; if it transfers everything to a Beyond; if it declares all earthly blessings to be valueless, and points exclusively to a world-shunning and contemplative life, it is an offence to all energetic, nay, ultimately, to all true natures; for such natures are certain that our faculties are given to us to be employed, and that the earth is assigned to us to be cultivated and subdued.

But is not the Gospel really a world-denying creed? Certain very well-known passages are appealed to which do not seem to admit of any other interpretation: "If thy right eye offend thee, pluck it out and cast it from thee"; "If thy right hand offend thee, cut it off"; or the answer to the rich young man: "Go sell what thou hast, and give to the poor, and thou shalt have treasure in heaven"; or the saying about those who have made themselves eunuchs for the kingdom of heaven's sake; or the utterance: "If any man come to me, and hate not his father, and mother, and wife, and children, and brethren, and sisters, yea, and his own life also, he cannot be my disciple." These and other passages seem to settle the matter, and to prove that the Gospel is altogether world-shunning and ascetic in its character. But to this thesis I oppose three considerations which point in another direction. The first is derived from the way in which Jesus came forward and from his manner and course of life; the second is based upon the impression which he made upon his disciples and was reflected in their own lives; the third springs from what we said about the fundamental feature of Jesus' message.

1. We find in our Gospels a remarkable utterance by Jesus, as follows: "John came neither eating nor drinking, and they say, He hath a devil. The Son of man came eating and drinking, and they say, Behold a man gluttonous and a wine-bibber." A glutton, then, and a wine-bibber was he called in addition to the other abusive names which were given him. From this it clearly follows that in his whole demeanour and manner of life he made an impression quite different from that of the preacher of repentance on the banks of the Jordan. Towards the various fields in which asceticism had been traditionally practised he must have taken up an attitude of indifference. We see him in the houses of the rich and of the poor, at meals, with women and amongst children; according to tradition even at a wedding. He allows his feet to be washed and his head to be anointed. Further, he is glad to lodge with Mary and Martha; he does not ask them to leave their home. When he finds to his joy people with a firm faith, he leaves them in the calling and the position in which they were. We do not hear of his telling them to sell all and follow him. Apparently he thinks it possible, nay, fitting that they should live unto their belief in the position in which God has placed them. His circle of disciples

is not exhausted by the few whom he summoned directly to follow him. He finds God's children everywhere; to discover them in their obscurity and to be allowed to speak to them some word of strength is his highest pleasure. But he did not organise his disciples into a band of monks, and he gave them no directions as to what they were to do and leave undone in the life of the day. No one who reads the Gospels with an unprejudiced mind, and does not pick his words, can fail to acknowledge that this free and active spirit does not appear to be bent under the yoke of asceticism, and that such words, therefore, as point in this direction must be taken in a rigid sense and generalised, but must not be regarded in a wider connexion and from a higher point of view.

2. It is certain that the disciples did not understand their master to be a world-shunning ascetic. We shall see later what sacrifices they made for the Gospel, and in what sense they renounced the world. But it is evident they did not give ascetic practices the chief place; they maintained the rule that the labourer is worthy of his hire; they did not send away their wives. We are incidentally told of Peter that his wife accompanied him on his missionary journeys. Apart from what we are told of an attempt to institute a kind of communism in the congregation at Jerusalem—and we may put it aside, as it is not trustworthy and, moreover, bore no ascetic character— we find nothing in the apostolic age which suggest a community of men who were ascetics on principle; on the contrary, we find the conviction prevailing elsewhere that it is within the given circumstances, in the calling and position in which he finds himself, that a man is to be a Christian. How differently things developed in Buddhism from the very start!

3. The all-important consideration is the third. Let me remind you of what we said in regard to Jesus' leading thoughts. In the sphere indicated by trust in God, humility, the forgiveness of sins and the love of one's neighbour, there is no room for the introduction of any other maxim, least of all for one of a legal character. At the same time Jesus makes it clear in what sense the kingdom of God is the antithesis of the world. The man who associates any ascetic practice with the words "Take

no thought," "Be merciful, even as your Father in heaven is merciful," and so on, and puts it upon the same level as those words, does not understand the sublime character of these sayings, and has either lost or has never attained the feeling that there is a union with God in which all such questions as shunning the world and asceticism are left far behind.

For these reasons we must decline to regard the Gospel as a message of world-denial.

On the other hand, Jesus speaks of three enemies, and the watchword which he gives in dealing with them is not that we are to flee them; rather he commands us to annihilate them. These three enemies are mammon, care, and selfishness. Observe that here there is no question of flight or denial, but of a battle which is to be fought until the enemy is annihilated; the forces of darkness are to be overthrown. By mammon he understands money and worldly goods in the widest sense of the word— worldly goods which try to gain the mastery over us, and make us tyrants over others; for money is "compressed force." Jesus speaks of this enemy as if it were a person, as if it were a knight in armour, or a king; nay, as if it were the devil himself. It is at this enemy that the saying "Ye cannot serve two masters" is aimed. Wherever anything belonging to the domain of mammon is of such value to a man that he sets his heart upon it, that he trembles at the thought of losing it, that he is no longer willing to give it up, such a man is already in bondage. Hence, when the Christian feels that this danger confronts him, he is not to treat with the enemy, but to fight, and not fight only but also destroy the mammon. Were Christ to preach among us to-day he would certainly not talk in general terms, and say to everyone, "give away everything you have"; but there are thousands among us to whom he would so speak, and that there is scarcely anyone who feels compelled to apply these sayings of the Gospel to himself is a fact that ought to make us suspicious.

The second enemy is care. At first sight it may surprise us that Jesus should describe care as so terrible a foe. He ranks it with "heathenism." It is true that in the Lord's Prayer he also taught men to pray, "Give us this day our daily bread"; but a confident request of this kind he does not call care. The care which he means is that which makes us timorous slaves of the day and of material things; the care through which bit by bit we fall a prey to the world. Care is to him an outrage on God, who preserves the very sparrows on the housetop; it destroys the fundamental relation with the Father in heaven, the child-like trust, and thus ruins our inmost soul. This is also a point in regard to which, as in respect to mammon, we must confess that we do not feel deeply and strongly enough to recognise the full truth of Jesus' message. But the question is, Who is right—he with the inexorable "Take no thought," or we with our debilitating fears? We, too, in a measure feel that a man is not really free, strong, and invincible, until he has put aside all his cares and cast them upon God. How much we could accomplish and how strong we should be, if we did not fret.

And then, thirdly : selfishness. It is self-denial, not asceticism, which Jesus requires; self-denial to the point of self-renuncia-tion. "If thy right eye offend thee, pluck it out; if thy right hand offend thee, cut it off." Wherever some desire of the senses gains the upper hand of you, so that you become coarse and vulgar, or in your selfishness a new master arises in you, you must destroy it; not because God has any pleasure in mutilation, but because you cannot otherwise preserve your better part. It is a hard demand. But it is not met by any act of general re-nunciation such as monks perform—the act may leave things just as they were before—but only by a struggle and a resolute renunciation at the critical point.

With all these enemies, mammon, care, and selfishness, what we have to exercise is *self-denial,* and therewith the relation of Christianity to asceticism is determined. Asceticism maintains the theory that all worldly blessings are in themselves of no value. This is not the theory to which we should be led if we were to go by the Gospel; "for the earth is the Lord's and the fulness thereof." But according to the Gospel a man is to ask : Can and ought I to regard property and honour, friends and relations, as blessings, or must I put them away? If certain of Jesus' sayings to this effect have been handed down to us in a general form and were, no doubt, so uttered, still they must be limited by the whole tenor of his discourses. What the Gospel asks of us is solemnly to examine ourselves, to maintain an earnest watch, and to destroy the enemy. There can be no doubt, however, that Jesus demanded self-denial and self-renunciation to a much greater extent than we like to think.

To sum up: Ascetic in the primary meaning of the word the Gospel is not; for it is a message of trust in God, of humility, of forgiveness of sin, and of mercy. This is a height which nothing else can approach, and into this sphere nothing else can force its way. Further, worldly blessings are not of the devil but of God—"Your heavenly Father knoweth that ye have need of all these things; he arrays the lilies of the field and feeds the fowls of the air." Asceticism has no place in the Gospel at all; what it asks is that we should struggle against mammon, against care, against selfishness; what it demands and disengages is *love*; the love that serves and is self-sacrificing. This struggle and this love are the kind of asceticism which the Gospel means, and whoever encumbers Jesus' message with any other kind fails to understand it. He fails to understand its grandeur and its importance; for there is something still more important than "giving one's body to be burned and bestowing all one's goods to feed the poor," namely, self-denial and love.

(2) *The Gospel and the poor, or the social question*

The bearings of the Gospel in regard to the social question form the second point which we propose to consider. It is closely akin to the first. Here also we encounter different views prevalent at the present moment, or, to be more exact, two views, which are mutually opposed. We are told, on the one hand, that the Gospel was in the main a great social message to the poor, and that everything else in it is of secondary importance —mere contemporary wrapping, ancient tradition, or new forms supplied by the first generations of Christians. Jesus, they say, was a great social reformer, who aimed at relieving the lower classes from the wretched condition in which they were languishing; he set up a social programme which embraced the equality of all men, relief from economical distress, and deliverance from misery and oppression. It is only so, they add, that he can be understood, and therefore so he was; or perhaps so he was, because it is only so that we can understand him. For years books and pamphlets have been written dealing with the Gospel in this sense; well-meant performances which aim at thus providing Jesus with a defence and a recommendation. But amongst those who take the Gospel to be an essentially social message there are also some who draw the opposite conclusion. By trying to prove that Jesus' message was wholly directed to bringing about an economical reform, they declare the Gospel to be an entirely Utopian and useless programme; the view, they say, which Jesus took of the world was gentle, but also weak; coming himself from the lower and oppressed classes, he shared the suspicion entertained by small people of the great and the rich; he abhorred all profitable trade and business; he failed to understand the necessity of acquiring wealth; and accordingly he shaped his programme so as to disseminate pauperism in the "world"—to him the world was Palestine—and then, by way of contrast with the misery on earth, to build up a kingdom in heaven; a programme unrealisable in itself, and offensive to men of energy. This, or something like this, is the view held by another section of those who identify the Gospel with a social message.

Opposed to this group of persons, united in the way in which they look at the Gospel but divided in their opinions in regard to it, there is another group upon whom it makes quite a different impression. They assert that as for any direct interest on Jesus' part in the economical and social conditions of his age; nay, further, as for any rudimentary interest in economical questions in general, it is only read into the Gospel, and that with economical questions the Gospel has absolutely nothing to do. Jesus, they say, certainly borrowed illustrations and examples from the domain of economics, and took a personal interest in the poor, the sick, and the miserable, but his purely religious teaching and his saving activity were in no way directed to any improvement in their earthly position : to say that his objects and intentions were of a social character is to secularise them. Nay, there are not a few among us who think him, like themselves, a "Conservative," who respected all these existing social differences and ordinances as "divinely ordained."

The voices which make themselves heard here are, as you will observe, very different, and the different points of view are defended with zeal and pertinacity. Now, if we are to try to find the position which corresponds to the facts, there is, first of all, a brief remark to be made on the age in which Jesus lived. Our knowledge of the social conditions in Palestine in his age and for some considerable time previously does not go very far; but there are certain leading features of it which we can establish, and two things more particularly which we can assert.

The governing classes, to which, above all, the Pharisees, and also the priests, belonged—the latter partly in alliance with the temporal rulers—had little feeling for the needs of the people. The condition of those classes may not have been much worse than it generally is at all times and in all nations, but it was bad. Moreover, there was here the additional circumstance that mercy and sympathy with the poor had been put into the background by devotion to public worship and to the cult of "righteousness." Oppression and tyranny on the part of the rich had long become a standing and inexhaustible theme with the Psalmists and with all men of any warm feelings. Jesus, too, could not have spoken of the rich as he did speak, unless they had grossly neglected their duties.

In the poor and oppressed classes, in the huge mass of want and evil, amongst the multitude of people for whom the word "misery" is often only another expression for the word "life," nay, is life itself—in this multitude there were groups of people at that time, as we can plainly see, who, with fervent and steadfast hope, were hanging upon the promises and consoling words of their God, waiting in humility and patience for the day when their deliverance was to come. Often too poor to pay even for the barest advantages and privileges of public worship, oppressed, thrust aside, and unjustly treated, they could not raise their eyes to the temple; but they looked to the God of Israel, and fervent prayers went up to him : "Watchman, what of the night?" Thus their hearts were opened to God and ready to receive him, and in many of the Psalms, and in the later Jewish literature akin to the Psalms, the word "poor" directly denotes those who have their hearts open and are waiting for the consolation of Israel. Jesus found this usage of speech in existence and adopted it. Therefore when we come across the expression "the poor" in the Gospels we must not think, without further ceremony, of the poor in the economic sense. As a matter of fact, poverty in the economic sense coincided to a large extent in those days with religious humility and an openness of the heart towards God, in contrast with the elevated "practice of virtue" of the Pharisees and its routine observance in "righteousness." But if this were the prevailing condition of affairs, then it is clear that our modern categories of "poor" and "rich" cannot be unreservedly transferred to that age. Yet we must not forget that in those days the economical sense was also, as a rule, included in the word "poor." We shall, therefore, have to examine in our next lecture the direction in which a distinction can be made, or perhaps to ask whether it is possible to fix the inner sense of Jesus' words in spite of the peculiar difficulty attaching to the conception of "poverty." We can have some confidence, however, that we shall not have to remain in obscurity on this point, for in its fundamental features the Gospel also throws a bright light upon the field covered by this question.

LECTURE SIX

At the close of the last lecture I referred to the problem presented by "the poor" in the Gospel. As a rule, the poor of whom Jesus was thinking were also those whose hearts are open towards God, and hence what is said of them cannot be applied without further ceremony to the poor generally. In considering the social question we must, therefore, put aside all those sayings of Jesus which obviously refer to the poor in the spiritual sense. These include, for instance, the first Beatitude, whether we accept it in the form in which it appears in Luke or in Matthew. The Beatitudes associated with it make it clear that Jesus was thinking of the poor whose hearts were inwardly open towards God. But, as we have no time to go through all the sayings separately, we must content ourselves with some leading considerations in order to establish the most important points.

Jesus regarded the possession of worldly goods as a grave danger for the soul, as hardening the heart, entangling us in earthly cares, and seducing us into a vulgar life of pleasure. "A rich man shall hardly enter the kingdom of heaven."

The contention that Jesus desired, so to speak, to bring about a general condition of poverty and distress, in order that he might afterwards make it the basis of his kingdom of heaven —a contention which we encounter in different forms—is erroneous. The very opposite is the case. Want he called want, and evil he called evil. Far from showing them any favour, he made the greatest and strongest efforts to combat and destroy them. In this sense, too, his whole activity was a saving activity, that is to say, a struggle against evil and against want. Nay, we might almost think that he over-estimated the depressing load of poverty and affliction; that he occupied himself too much with it; and that, taking the moral bearings of life as a whole, he attributed too great an importance to those forces of

sympathy and mercy which are expected to counteract this
state of things. But neither, of course, would this view be correct.
He knows of a power which he thinks still worse than want
and misery, namely, sin; and he knows of a force still more
emancipating than mercy, namely, forgiveness. His discourses
and actions leave no doubt upon this point. It is certain, therefore, that Jesus never and nowhere wished to keep up poverty
and misery, but, on the contrary, he combated them himself
and bade others combat them. The Christians who in the course
of the Church's history were for countenancing mendicancy
and recommending universal pauperisation, or sentimentally
coquetted with misery and distress, cannot with any show of
reason appeal to him. Upon those, however, who were anxious
to devote their whole lives to the preaching of the Gospel and
the ministry of the Word—he did not ask this of everyone,
but regarded it as a special calling from God and a special gift
—upon them he enjoined the renunciation of all that they had,
that is to say, all worldly goods. Yet that does not mean that
he relegated them to a life of beggary. On the contrary, they
were to be certain that they would find their bread and their
means of livelihood. What he meant by that we learn from a
saying of his which was accidentally omitted from the Gospels,
but has been handed down to us by the apostle Paul. In the
ninth chapter of his first epistle to the Corinthians he writes:
"The Lord hath ordained that they which preach the gospel
should live of the gospel." An absence of worldly possessions
he required of the ministers of the Word, that is, of the missionaries, in order that they might live entirely for their calling. But
he did not mean that they were to beg. This is a Franciscan
misconception which is perhaps suggested by Jesus' words but
carries us away from his meaning.

In this connexion allow me to digress for a moment from our
subject. Those members of the Christian Churches who have
become professional evangelists or ministers of the Word in their
parishes have not, as a rule, found it necessary to follow the
Lord's injunction to dispossess themselves of their worldly goods.
So far as priests or pastors, as the case may be, and not missionaries, are concerned, it may be said with some justice that the

injunction does not refer to them; for it presupposes that a man has undertaken the office of *propagating* the Gospel. It may be said, further, that the Lord's injunctions, over and above those relating to the commandment of love, must not be made into inviolable laws, as otherwise Christian liberty will be impaired, and the high privilege of the Christian religion to adapt its shape to the course of history, free from all constraint, will be prejudiced. But still it may be asked whether it would not have been an extraordinary gain to Christianity if those who are called to be its ministers—the missionaries and pastors—had followed the Lord's rules. At the very least, it ought to be a strict principle with them to concern themselves with property and worldly goods only so far as will prevent them being a burden to others, and beyond that to renounce them. I entertain no doubt that the time will come when the world will tolerate a life of luxury among those who are charged with the cure of souls as little as it tolerates priestly government. Our feelings in this respect are becoming finer, and that is an advantage. It will no longer be thought fitting, in the higher sense of the word, for anyone to preach resignation and contentment to the poor who is well off himself, and zealously concerned for the increase of his property. A healthy man may well offer consolation to the sick; but how shall a man of property convince those who have none that worldly goods are of no value? The Lord's injunction that the minister of the Word is to divest himself of worldly possessions will still come to be honoured in the history of his communion.

Jesus laid down no social programme for the suppression of poverty and distress, if by programme we mean a set of definitely prescribed regulations. With economical conditions and contemporary circumstances he did not interfere. Had he become entangled in them; had he given laws which were ever so salutary for Palestine, what would have been gained by it? They would have served the needs of a day, and tomorrow would have been antiquated; to the Gospel they would have been a burden and a source of confusion. We must be careful not to exceed the limits set to such injunctions as "Give to him that asketh thee," and others of a similar kind. They must be

understood in connexion with the time and the situation. They
refer to the immediate wants of the applicant, which were
satisfied with a piece of bread, a drink of water, an article of
clothing to cover his nakedness. We must remember that in the
Gospel we are in the East, and in circumstances which from
an economical point of view are somewhat undeveloped. Jesus
was no social reformer. He could say on occasion, "The poor
ye have always with you," and thereby, it seems, indicate that
the conditions would undergo no essential change. He refused
to be a judge between contending heirs, and a thousand
problems of economics and social life he would have just as
resolutely put aside as the unreasonable demand that he would
settle a question of inheritance. Yet again and again people
have ventured to deduce some concrete social programme from
the Gospel. Even Protestant theologians have made the attempt,
and are still making it—an endeavour hopeless in itself and
full of danger, but absolutely bewildering and intolerable when
people try to "fill up the gaps"—and they are many—to be
found in the Gospel with regulations and programmes drawn
from the Old Testament.

No religion, not even Buddhism, ever went to work with
such an energetic social message, and so strongly identified itself
with that message as we see to be the case in the Gospel. How
so? Because the words "Love thy neighbour as thyself" were
spoken in deep earnest; because with these words Jesus turned
a light upon all the concrete relations of life, upon the world
of hunger, poverty and misery; because, lastly, he uttered them
as a religious, nay, as *the* religious maxim. Let me remind you
once more of the parable of the Last Judgment, where the
whole question of a man's worth and destiny is made dependent
on whether he has practised the love of his neighbour; let me
remind you of the other parable of the rich man and poor
Lazarus. I should like to cite another story, too, which is little
known, because it occurs in this wording, not in our four
Gospels but in the Gospel of the Hebrews. The story of the
rich young man is there handed down as follows: "A rich
man said to the Lord: Master, what good must I do that I
may have life? He answered him: Man, keep the law and the

prophets. The other answered : That have I done. He said to
him : Go, sell all thy possessions and distribute them to the poor,
and come and follow me. Then the rich man began to scratch
his head, and the speech did not please him. And the Lord said
to him : How canst thou say, I have kept the law and the
prophets, as it is written in the law, Love thy neighbour as
thyself? Behold, many of thy brethren, sons of Abraham, lie in
dirty rags and die of hunger, and thy house is full of many
goods, and nothing comes out of it to them." You observe how
Jesus felt the material wants of the poor, and how he deduced
a remedy for such distress from the commandment : "Love thy
neighbour as thyself." People ought not to speak of loving their
neighbours if they can allow men beside them to starve and die
in misery. It is not only that the Gospel preaches solidarity
and the helping of others; it is in this message that its real im-
port consists. In this sense it is profoundly socialistic, just as it
is also profoundly individualistic, because it establishes the
infinite and independent value of every human soul. Its
tendency to union and brotherliness is not so much an accidental
phenomenon in its history as the essential feature of its character.
The Gospel aims at founding a community among men as wide
as human life itself and as deep as human need. As has been
truly said, its object is to transform the socialism which rests
on the basis of conflicting interests into the socialism which rests
on the consciousness of a spiritual unity. In this sense its social
message can never be outbid. In the course of the ages people's
opinions as to what constitutes "an existence worthy of a man"
have, thank God, become much changed and improved. But
Jesus, too, knew of this way of measuring things. Did he not
once refer, almost bitterly, to his own position : "The foxes have
holes and the birds of the air have nests : but the Son of man
hath not where to lay his head"? A dwelling, sufficient daily
bread, cleanliness—all these needs he touched upon, and their
satisfaction he held to be necessary, and a condition of earthly
life. If a man cannot procure them for himself, others are to
step in and do it for him. There can be no doubt, therefore, that
if Jesus were with us to-day he would side with those who are
making great efforts to relieve the hard lot of the poor and

procure them better conditions of life. The fallacious principle
of the free play of forces, of the "live and let live" principle—
a better name for it would be "live and let die"—is entirely
opposed to the Gospel. And it is not as our servants, but as our
brothers, that we are to help the poor.

Lastly, our riches do not belong to us alone. The Gospel has
prescribed no regulations as to how we are to use them, but it
leaves us in no doubt that we are to regard ourselves, not as
owners but as administrators in the service of our neighbour.
Nay, it almost looks as if Jesus contemplated the possibility of
a union among men in which wealth, as private property in the
strict sense of the word, was non-existent. Here, however, we
touch upon a question which is not easy to decide, and which,
perhaps, ought not to be raised at all, because Jesus' eschatological ideas and his particular horizon enter into it. Nor is it a
question that we need raise. It is the disposition which Jesus
kindled in his disciples towards poverty and want that is all-
important.

The Gospel is a social message, solemn and over-powering
in its force; it is the proclamation of solidarity and brotherliness, in favour of the poor. But the message is bound up with
the recognition of the infinite value of the human soul, and
is contained in what Jesus said about the kingdom of God.
We may also assert that it is an essential part of what he there
said. But laws or ordinances or injunctions bidding us forcibly
alter the conditions of the age in which we may happen to be
living are not to be found in the Gospel.

(3) *The Gospel and the law, or the question of public order*

The problem dealing with the relation of the Gospel to law
embraces two leading questions: (1) the relation of the Gospel
to constituted authority; (2) the relation of the Gospel to legal
ordinances generally, in so far as they possess a wider range
than is covered by the conception "constituted authority." It
is not easy to mistake the answer to the first question, but the
second is more complicated and beset with greater difficulties;
and very diverse opinions are entertained in regard to it.

As to Jesus' relation to the constituted authorities of his day, I need scarcely remind you again in express terms that he was no political revolutionary, and that he laid down no political programme. Although he is sure that his Father would send him twelve legions of angels were he to ask Him, he did not ask Him. When they wanted to make him a king, he disappeared. Ultimately, indeed, when he thought well to reveal himself to the whole nation as the Messiah—how he came to the decision and carried it out, are points in which we are left in the dark—he made his entry into Jerusalem as a king; but of the modes of presenting himself which prophecy suggested, he chose that which was most remote from a political manifestation. The way in which he understood his Messianic duty is shown by his driving the buyers and sellers from the temple. In this cleansing of the temple it was not the constituted authorities whom he attacked, but those who had assumed to themselves rights of authority over the soul. In every nation, side by side with constituted authorities an unconstituted authority is established, or rather two constituted authorities. They are the political church and the political parties. What the political church wants, in the widest sense of the word and under very various guises, is to rule; to get hold of men's souls and bodies, consciences and worldly goods. What political parties want is the same; and when the heads of these parties set themselves up as popular leaders, a terrorism is developed which is often worse than the fear of royal despots. It was not otherwise in Palestine in Jesus' day. The priests and the Pharisees held the nation in bondage and murdered its soul. For this unconstituted "authority" Jesus showed a really emancipating and refreshing disrespect. He was never tired of attacking it—nay, in his struggle with it he roused himself to a state of holy indignation —of exposing its wolfish nature and hypocrisy, and of declaring that its day of judgment was at hand. In whatever domain it had any warrant to act, he accepted it: "Go and show yourselves unto the priests." So far as they really proclaimed God's law he recognised them: "Whatever they tell you to do, that do." But these were the people to whom he read the terrible lecture given in Matt. xxiii. 27: "Woe unto you scribes and

Pharisees, hypocrites! for ye are like unto whited sepulchres, which indeed appear beautiful outward, but are within full of dead men's bones and of all uncleanness." Towards these spiritual "authorities," then, he filled his disciples with a holy want of respect, and even of "King" Herod he spoke with bitter irony: "Go ye and tell that fox." On the other hand, so far as we can judge from the scanty evidence before us, his attitude towards the real authorities, those who wielded the sword, was different. He recognised that they had an actual right to be obeyed, and he never withdrew his own person from their jurisdiction. Nor are we to understand the commandment against swearing as including an oath taken before a magistrate. No one with a grain of salt, as Wellhausen has rightly said, can miss the inner meaning of this commandment. On the other hand, we must be careful not to rate Jesus' position in regard to constituted authority too high. People usually appeal to the often quoted saying: "Render unto Cæsar the things which are Cæsar's, and unto God the things that are God's." But this saying is often misunderstood. Whenever it is explained as meaning that Jesus recognised God and Cæsar as the two powers which in some way or other exist side by side, or are even in secret alliance, it is taken in a wrong sense. Jesus had no such thought; on the contrary, he spoke of the two powers as separate and divorced from each other. God and Cæsar are the lords of two quite different provinces. Jesus settled the question that was in dispute by pointing out this difference, which is so great that no conflict between the powers can arise. The penny is an earthly coin and bears Cæsar's image; let it be given, then, to Cæsar, but—this we may take as the complement—the soul and all its powers have nothing to do with Cæsar; they belong to God. In a word, the all-important matter, in Jesus' view, is not to mix up the two provinces. When we are once quite clear about this, then we may go on to remark on the significance of the fact that Jesus enjoined compliance with the demand for payment of the imperial taxes. No doubt it is important to note that he himself respected the constituted authorities, and wished to see them respected; but in regard

to the estimate which he formed of them, his language, to say
the least, is of a neutral character.

On the other hand, we possess another saying of Jesus in
regard to constituted authority which is much less often quoted,
and nevertheless affords us a deeper insight into the Lord's
thoughts than the one which we have just discussed. Let us
consider it for a moment. The fact that it forms a point of
transition to the consideration of the attitude which Jesus took
up in regard to legal regulations in general also makes it worth
our attention. In Mark x. 42 we read: "Jesus called them
(i.e. his disciples) to him and saith unto them, Ye know that
they which are accounted to rule over the Gentiles exercise
lordship over them: and their great ones exercise authority
upon them. But so shall it not be among you: but whosoever
shall be great among you shall be your minister: and whosoever
of you will be the chiefest shall be servant of all." Observe here,
first of all, the "transvaluation of values." Jesus simply reverses
the usual process: to be great and to occupy the foremost
position means, in his view, to serve; his disciples are to aim,
not at ruling, but at each being all other men's servant. Next
observe the opinion which he has of authority as it was then
constituted. Their functions are based on *force,* and this is the
very reason which, in Jesus' view, puts them outside the moral
sphere; nay, there is a fundamental opposition between it and
them: "Thus do the earthly rulers." Jesus tells his disciples to
act differently. Law and legal ordinance, as resting on force
only, on actual power and its exercise, have no moral value.
Nevertheless Jesus did not command men not to subject themselves to these authorities; they were to rate them according to
their value, that is, according to their non-value, and they were
to arrange their own lives on other principles, namely, on the
opposite; they were not to use force, but to serve. Here we have
already passed to the general ground of legal ordinance, for it
seems to be an essential feature of all law to secure observance
by force when called in question.

When we approach the second point, the relation of the Gospel
to legal ordinance generally, we again encounter two different
views. One of them—in modern times more particularly

maintained, in his treatise on Canon Law, by Prof. Sohm
of Leipzig, who presents points of contact with Tolstoi—lays
down that in their respective natures law and the world of
spiritual things are diametrically opposed; and that it is in
contradiction with the character of the Gospel and the community founded thereon that the Church has developed any
legal ordinances at all. In his survey of the earliest development of the Church Prof. Sohm has gone so far as to see in
the moment when Christendom gave a place in its midst to
legal ordinances a second Fall. Nevertheless he is unwilling to
impugn the law in its own province. But Tolstoi refuses, in the
name of the Gospel, to allow the law any rights at all. He maintains that the leading principle of the Gospel is that a man is
never to insist upon his rights, and that not even constituted
authority is to offer any external resistance to evil. Authority
and law are simply to cease. Opposed to Tolstoi there are
others who more or less positively contend that the Gospel takes
law and legal relations under its protection; that it sanctifies
them and thereby raises them into a divine sphere. These are,
briefly, the two leading points of view which are here in conflict.

As regards the latter, there is little that need be said. It is a
mockery of the Gospel to say that it protects and sanctifies
everything that presents itself as law and legal relation at a
given moment. Leaving a thing alone and bearing with it are
not the same as sanctioning and preserving it. Nay, it is a serious
question whether even bearing with it is not too much to say,
and whether Tolstoi is not right. The difficulty of the matter
makes it necessary that I should take you back a little way in
Jewish history.

For hundreds of years the poor and oppressed in the people
of Israel had been crying out for justice. It was a cry which still
moves us to-day as we hear it in the words of the prophets and
out of the prayers of the Psalmists; but time after time it passed
unheeded. None of the legal regulations in force was free from
the power of tyrannical authorities, to be distorted and exploited
by them just as they saw fit. In speaking of legal regulations
and their exercise, and in examining Jesus' attitude towards
them, we must not straightway think of our own legal regulations,

which have grown up partly on the basis of Christianity. Jesus was of a nation the greater part of which had for generations been in vain asking for their rights, and which was familiar with law only in the form of force. The necessary consequence was that in such a nation a feeling of despair arose in regard to the law; despair, as much of the possibility of ever getting justice on earth, as, conversely, of the moral claim of law to have any validity at all. We can see something of this temper even in the Gospel. But there is a second consideration which is a standing corrective to this temper. Jesus, like all truly religious minds, was firmly convinced that in the end God will do justice. If He does not do it here, He will do it in the Beyond, and that is the main point. In this connexion there was, in Jesus' view, nothing objectionable in the idea of law in the sense of a just recompense; it was a lofty, nay, a dominating idea. Just recompense is the function of God's majesty; to what extent it is modified by His mercy is a question which we need not here consider. The contention that Jesus took a disparaging view of law as such, and of the exercise of law, cannot be sustained for a moment. On the contrary, everyone is to get his rights; nay more, his disciples are one day to share in administering God's justice and themselves judge. It was only the justice which was exercised with violence and therefore unjustly, the justice which lay upon the nation like a tyrannical and bloody decree, that he set aside. He believed in true justice, and he was certain, too, that it would prevail; so certain, that he did not think it necessary for justice to use force in order to remain justice.

This brings us to the last point. We possess a number of Jesus' sayings in which he directs his disciples to renounce all their lawful demands, and so forgo their just rights. You all know those sayings. Let me remind you of one only: "But I say unto you, That ye resist not evil, but whosoever shall smite thee on thy right cheek, turn to him the other also. And if any man will sue thee at the law, and take away thy coat, let him have thy cloak also." The demand here made seems to proscribe law and disorganise all the legal relations of life. Again and again these words have been appealed to with the object of showing either that Christianity is incompatible with life as it actually is, or that Christendom has fallen away from the principles of its Master. By way of reply to this argument the following observations may be made: (i) Jesus was, as we have seen, steeped in the conviction that God does justice; in the end, therefore, the oppressor will not prevail and the oppressed will get his rights. (ii) Earthly rights are in themselves of little account, and it does not much matter if we lose them. (iii) The world is in such an unhappy state, injustice has got so much the upper hand in it, that the victim of oppression is incapable of making good his rights even if he tries. (iv) As God—and this is the main point—mingles His justice with mercy, and lets His sun shine on the just and on the unjust, so Jesus' disciple is to show love to his enemies and disarm them by gentleness. Such are the thoughts which underlie those lofty sayings and at the same time set them their due limits. And is the demand which they contain really so supramundane, so impossible? Do we not in the circle of our family and friends advise those who belong to us to act in the same way, and not to return evil for evil and abuse for abuse? What family, what society, could continue to exist, if every member of it were anxious only to pursue his own rights, and did not learn to renounce them even when attacked? Jesus regards his disciples as a circle of friends, and he looks out beyond this circle to a league of brothers which will take shape in the future and extend. But, we are asked, are we in all cases to renounce the pursuit of our rights in the face of our enemies? are we to use no weapons but those of gentleness? To speak with Tolstoi, are the magistrates not to inflict punishment, and thereby to be effaced? are nations not to fight for house and home when they are wantonly attacked? I venture to maintain that when Jesus spoke the words which I have quoted, he was not thinking of such cases, and that to interpret them in this direction involves a clumsy and dangerous misconception of their meaning. Jesus never had anyone but the individual in mind, and the abiding disposition of the heart in love. To say that this disposition cannot coexist with the pursuit of one's own rights, with the conscientious administration of justice, and with the stern punishment of crime, is a

piece of prejudice, in support of which we may appeal in vain
to the letter of those sayings, which did not aim at being laws
—that is, at prescribing regulations. This much, however, must
be added, in order that the loftiness of the demand which the
Gospel makes may be in no way abated : Jesus' disciple ought
to be able to renounce the pursuit of his rights, and ought to
co-operate in forming a nation of brothers, in which justice is
done no longer by the aid of force, but by free obedience to
the good, and which is united, not by legal regulations, but
by the ministry of love.

LECTURE SEVEN

WE WERE occupied in the last lecture with the relation of the Gospel to law and legal ordinance. We saw that Jesus was convinced that God does, and will do, justice. We saw, further, that he demanded of his disciples that they should be able to renounce their rights. In giving expression to this demand, far from having all the circumstances of his own time in mind, still less the more complex conditions of a later age, he has one and one only present to his soul, namely, the relation of every man to the kingdom of God. Because a man is to sell all that he has in order to buy the pearl of great price, so he must also be able to abandon his earthly rights and subordinate everything to that highest relation. But in connexion with this message of his, Jesus opens up to us the prospect of a union among men, which is held together, not by any legal ordinance, but by the rule of love, and where a man conquers his enemy by gentleness. It is a high and glorious ideal, and we have received it from the very foundation of our religion. It ought to float before our eyes as the goal and guiding star of our historical development. Whether mankind will ever attain to it, who can say? but we can and ought to approximate to it, and in these days—otherwise than two or three hundred years ago—we feel a moral obligation in this direction. Those of us who possess more delicate and therefore more prophetic perceptions no longer regard the kingdom of love and peace as a mere Utopia.

But for this very reason there are many among us to-day upon whom a very serious and difficult question presses with redoubled force. We see a whole class struggling for its rights; or, rather, we see it struggling to extend and increase its rights. Is that compatible with the Christian temper? Does not the Gospel forbid such a struggle? Have we not been told that we are to renounce the rights we have, to say nothing of trying to get more? Must we, then, as Christians, recall the labouring classes from the struggle for their rights, and exhort them only to patience and submission?

The problem with which we have here to do is also stated more or less in the form of an accusation against Christianity. Earnest men in political circles of a socialistic tendency, who would gladly be guided by Jesus Christ, complain that in this matter the Gospel leaves them in the lurch. They say that it imposes restraint upon aspirations which with a clear conscience they feel to be justified; that in requiring absolute meekness and submission it disarms everyone who wants to fight; that it narcotises, as it were, all real energy. Some say this with pain and regret, others with satisfaction. The latter assert that they always knew that the Gospel was not for the healthy and the strong, but for the broken-down; that it knows, and wants to know, nothing of the fact that life, and especially modern life, is a struggle, a struggle for one's own rights. What answer are we to give them?

My own opinion is that these statements and complaints are made by people who have never yet clearly realised with what the Gospel is concerned, and who rashly and improperly connect it with earthly things. The Gospel makes its appeal to the inner man, who, whether he is healthy or sick, in a happy position or a miserable, obliged to spend his earthly life fighting or quietly maintaining what he has won, always remains the same. "My kingdom is not of this world"; it is no earthly kingdom that the Gospel establishes. Not only are these words inconsistent with such a political theocracy as the Pope aims at setting up and with all worldly dominion; they go much further, and forbid all direct and formal interference of religion in worldly affairs. What the Gospel does say is this: Whoever you may be, and whatever your position, whether bondman or free, whether fighting or at rest—your real business in life is always the same. There is only *one* relation and *one* idea which you must not violate, and in the face of which all others are only varied trappings and vain show: to be a child of God and a citizen of His kingdom, and to exercise love. How you are to maintain yourself in this life on earth, and in what way you are to serve your neighbour, is left to you and your own liberty of action. This is what the apostle Paul understood by the Gospel, and I do not believe that he misunderstood it. Then let us fight, let us struggle, let us get justice for the oppressed, let us order the circumstances of the world as we with a clear conscience can, and as we may think best for our neighbour; but do not let us expect the Gospel to afford us any direct help; let us make no selfish demands for ourselves; and let us not forget that the world passes away, not only with the lusts thereof, but also with its regulations and its goods! Once more be it said: the Gospel knows only one goal, one idea; and it demands of a man that he shall never put them aside. If the exhortation to renounce takes, in any narrow and austere way, a foremost place in Jesus' words, it is to impress upon us the paramount and exclusive claims of the relation to God and the idea of love. The Gospel is above all questions of mundane development; it is concerned not with material things but with the souls of men.

With this we have already passed to the next question which was to occupy our attention, and we have half answered it.

(4) The Gospel and work, or the question of civilisation

The points which we shall have to consider here are essentially the same as those which we emphasised in regard to the question just discussed; and we shall therefore be able to proceed more concisely.

Jesus' teaching has been felt again and again, but above all in our own day, to exhibit no interest in any systematic work or calling, and no appreciation of those ideal possessions which go by the name of Art and Science. Nowhere, people say, does Jesus summon men to labour and to put their hands to the work of progress; in vain shall we look in his words for any expression of pleasure in vigorous activity; these ideal possessions lay far beyond his field of vision. In that last unhappy book of his, *The Old Faith and the New*, David Friedrich Strauss gave particularly harsh expression to this feeling. He speaks of a

fundamental defect in the Gospel, which he considers antiquated and useless because out of sympathy with the progress of
civilisation. But long before Strauss the Pietistic movement
exhibited the same sort of feeling. The Pietists tried to evade
the difficulty in a way of their own. They started from the
position that Jesus must be able to serve as a direct example
for all men, whatever their calling; must have proved his
capacity in all the situations in which a man can be placed. They
admitted that a cursory examination of Jesus' life disclosed
the fact that this requirement was not fulfilled; but they were of
opinion that on a closer inspection it would be found that he
was really the best bricklayer, the best tailor, the best judge,
the best scholar, and so on, and that he had the best knowledge
and understanding of everything. They turned and twisted what
Jesus said and did until it was made to express and corroborate
what they wanted. Although it was a childish attempt that they
made, the problem of which they were sensible was nevertheless
of some moment. They felt that their consciences and their
callings bound them to a definite activity and a definite business;
they were clear that they ought not to become monks; and yet
they were anxious to practise the imitation of Christ in the full
sense. They felt, then, that he must have stood in the same
situation as they themselves, and that his horizon must have
been the same as theirs.

Here we have the same case as we dealt with in the last
section, only covering a wider field. Again and again the error
recurs that the Gospel has to do with the affairs of the world,
and that it is its business to prescribe how they are to be carried
on. Here, too, the old and almost ineradicable tendency of
mankind to rid itself of its freedom and responsibility in higher
things and subject itself to a law, comes into play. It is much
easier, in fact, to resign oneself to any, even the sternest, kind
of authority, than to live in the liberty of the good. But putting
this aside, the question remains : Is it not a real defect in the
Gospel that it betrays so little sympathy with the business of
life, and is out of touch with the *humaniora* in the sense of
knowledge, art, and civilisation generally?

I answer, in the first place : What would have been gained

if it had not possessed this "defect"? Suppose that it had taken
an active interest in all those efforts, would it not have become
entangled in them, or, at any rate, have incurred the risk of
appearing to be so entangled? Labour, art, science, the progress
of civilisation—these are not things which exist in the abstract;
they exist in the particular phase of an age. The Gospel, then,
would have to ally itself with them. But phases change. In the
Roman Church of to-day we see how heavily religion is
burdened by being connected with a particular epoch of civilisation. In the Middle Ages this Church, anxious to participate
to the full in all questions of progress and civilisation, gave them
form and shape, and laid down their laws. Insensibly, however,
the Church identified its sacred inheritance and its peculiar
mission with the knowledge, the maxims, and the interests which
it then acquired; so that it is now, as it were, firmly pinned
down to the philosophy, the political economy, in short, to the
whole civilisation, of the Middle Ages. On the other hand, what
a service the Gospel has rendered to mankind by having
sounded the notes of religion in mighty chords and banished
every other melody!

In the second place, labour and the progress of civilisation
are, no doubt, very precious, and summon us to strenuous
exertion. But they do not comprise the highest ideal. They are
incapable of filling the soul with real satisfaction. Although
work may give pleasure, that is only one aspect of the matter. I
have always found that the people who talk loudest about the
pleasure which work affords make no very great effort themselves; whilst those who are uninterruptedly engaged in heavy
labour are hesitating in its praises. As a matter of fact, there is
a great deal of hypocritical twaddle talked about work. Three-
fourths of it and more is nothing but stupefying toil, and the
man who really works hard shares the poet's aspirations as he
looks forward to the evening :

Head, hands, and feet rejoice: the work is done.

And, then, think of the results of all this labour! When a
man has done a piece of work, he would like to do it over again,

and the knowledge of its defects falls heavily on soul and conscience. No! it is not in so far as we work that we live, but in so far as we rejoice in the love of others, and ourselves exercise love. Faust is right: Labour which is labour and nothing else becomes an aversion. We long for the streams of living water, and for the spring itself from which those waters flow:

> *Man sehnt sich nach des Lebens Bächen,*
> *Ach! nach des Lebens Quelle hin.*

Labour is a valuable safety-valve and useful in keeping off greater ills, but it is not in itself an absolute good, and we cannot include it amongst our ideals. The same may be said of the progress of civilisation. It is of course to be welcomed; but the piece of progress in which we delight to-day becomes something mechanical by to-morrow, and leaves us cold. The man of any deep feeling will thankfully receive anything that the development of progress may bring him; but he knows very well that his situation inwardly—the problems that agitate him and the fundamental position in which he stands—is not essentially, nay, is scarcely even unessentially, altered by it all. It is only for a moment that it seems as if something new were coming, and a man were being really relieved of his burden. Gentlemen, when a man grows older and sees more deeply into life, he does not find, if he possesses any inner world at all, that he is advanced by the external march of things, by "the progress of civilisation." Nay, he feels himself, rather, where he was before, and forced to seek the sources of strength which his forefathers also sought. He is forced to make himself a native of the kingdom of God, the kingdom of the Eternal, the kingdom of Love; and he comes to understand that it was only of this kingdom that Jesus Christ desired to speak and to testify, and he is grateful to him for it.

But, in the third place, Jesus had a strong and positive conviction of the aggressive and forward character of his message. "I am come to send fire on the earth, and"—he added—"what will I if it be already kindled?" The fire of the judgment and the forces of love were what he wanted to call forth, in order to create a new humanity. If he spoke of these forces of love in the simple manner corresponding to the conditions nearest at hand —the feeding of the hungry, the clothing of the naked, the visiting of the sick and those in prison—it is nevertheless clear that a great inward transformation of the humanity which he saw in the mirror of the little nation in Palestine hovered before his eyes: "One is your master, and all ye are brethren." The last hour is come; but in the last hour from a small seed a tree is to grow up which shall spread its branches far and wide. Further, he was revealing the knowledge of God, and he was certain that it would ripen the young, strengthen the weak, and make them God's champions. Knowledge of God is the spring that is to fructify the barren field, and pour forth streams of living water. In this sense he spoke of it as the highest and the only necessary good, as the condition of all edification, and, we may also say, of all true growth and progress. Lastly, he saw on his horizon not only the judgment, but also a kingdom of justice, of love, and of peace, which, though it came from heaven, was nevertheless for this earth. When it is to come, he himself knows not—the hour is known to the Father only; but he knows how and by what means it will spread; and side by side with the highly-coloured, dramatic pictures which pass through his soul he has a quiet vision of things that are fixed and steady; he sees the vineyard of God on this earth and God calling His labourers into it—happy the man who receives a call!—he sees them working in the vineyard, standing no longer idle in the market-place, and at last receiving their reward. Or take the parable of the talents distributed in order to be employed, and therefore not to be buried in a napkin. A day's work, labour, increase, progress—he sees it all, but placed at the service of God and neighbour, encircled by the light of the Eternal, and removed from the service of transient things.

To sum up what we have here tried to indicate. Is the complaint from which we started at the beginning of this section justified? Ought we really to desire that the Gospel had adapted itself to "the progress of civilisation"? Here, too, I think, we have to learn from the Gospel and not to find fault with it. It tells us of the real work which humanity has to accomplish, and we ought not to meet its message by entrenching ourselves behind our miserable "work of civilisation." "The image of Christ," as a modern historian justly says, "remains the sole basis of all moral culture, and in the measure in which it succeeds in making its light penetrate is the moral culture of the nations increased or diminished."

(5) *The Gospel and the Son of God, or the Christological question*

We now pass from the group of questions of which we have been treating hitherto. There were four of them, all intimately connected with one another. Failure to answer them rightly always proceeds from not rating the Gospel high enough; from somehow or other dragging it down to the level of mundane questions and entangling it in them. Or, to put the matter differently: The forces of the Gospel appeal to the deepest foundations of human existence and to them only; it is there alone that their leverage is applied. If a man is unable, then, to go down to the root of humanity, and has no feeling for it and no knowledge of it, he will fail to understand the Gospel, and will then try to profane it or else complain that it is of no use.

We now, however, approach quite a different problem: What position did Jesus himself take up towards the Gospel while he was proclaiming it, and how did he wish himself to be accepted? We are not yet dealing with the way in which his disciples accepted him, or the place which they gave him in their hearts, and the opinion which they formed of him; we are now speaking only of his own testimony of himself. But the question is one which lands us in the great sphere of controverted questions which cover the history of the Church from the first century up to our own time. In the course of this controversy men put an end to brotherly fellowship for the sake of a *nuance*; and thousands were cast out, condemned, loaded with chains and done to death. It is a gruesome story. On the question of "Christology" men beat their religious doctrines into terrible weapons, and spread fear and intimidation everywhere. This attitude still continues; Christology is treated as though the Gospel had no other problem to offer, and the accompanying fanaticism is still rampant in our own day. Who can wonder at the difficulty of the problem, weighed down as it is with such a burden of history and made the sport of parties? Yet anyone who will look at our Gospels with unprejudiced eyes will not find that the question of Jesus' own testimony is insoluble. So much of it, however, as remains obscure and mysterious to our minds ought to remain so; as Jesus meant it to be, and as in the very nature of the problem it is. It is only in pictures that we can give it expression. "There are phenomena which cannot, without the aid of symbols, be brought within the range of the understanding."

Before we examine Jesus' own testimony about himself, two leading points must be established. In the first place, he desired no other belief in his person and no other attachment to it than is contained in the keeping of his commandments. Even with the fourth evangelist, who often seems to raise Jesus' person above the contents of the Gospel, the idea is still clearly formulated: "If ye love me, keep my commandments." He must himself have found, during his labours, that some people honoured, nay, even trusted him, without troubling themselves about the contents of his message. It was to them that he addressed the reprimand: "Not every one that saith unto me, Lord, Lord, shall enter into the kingdom of heaven; but he that doeth the will of my Father." To lay down any "doctrine" about his person and his dignity independently of the Gospel was, then, quite outside his sphere of ideas. In the second place, he described the Lord of heaven and earth as his God and his Father; as the Creator, and as Him who is alone good. He is certain that everything which he has and everything which he is to accomplish comes from this Father. He prays to Him; he subjects himself to His will; he struggles hard to find out what it is and to fulfil it. Aim, strength, understanding, the issue, and the hard *must*, all come from the Father. This is what the Gospels say, and it cannot be turned and twisted. This feeling, praying, working, struggling and suffering individual is a man who in the face of his God also associates himself with other men.

These two facts mark out, as it were, the boundaries of the ground covered by Jesus' testimony of himself. They do not, it is true, give us any positive information as to what he said; but we shall understand what he really meant by his testimony if we look closely at the two descriptions which he gave of himself; the *Son of God* and the *Messiah* (the Son of David, the Son of Man).

The first designation, "the Son of God," Messianic though it may have been in its original conception, lies very much nearer to our modern way of thinking than the second, for Jesus himself gave a meaning to this conception which almost takes it out of the class of Messianic ideas, or at all events does not make its inclusion in that class necessary to a proper understanding of it. On the other hand, unless we are willing to be content with a dead word, the designation "the Messiah" is at first blush one that is quite foreign to our ideas. Without some explanation we cannot understand—nay, unless we are Jews, we cannot understand at all—what this dignity means and what rank and character it possesses. It is only when we have ascertained its meaning by historical study that we can ask whether the word has a significance which in any way survives the destruction of the husk in which it took shape in Jewish political life.

Let us first of all consider the designation, "Son of God." Jesus in one of his discourses made it specially clear why and in what sense he gave himself this name. The saying is to be found in Matthew, and not, as might perhaps have been expected, in John: "No man knoweth the Son but the Father; neither knoweth any man the Father, save the Son, and he to whomsoever the Son will reveal him." It is "knowledge of God" that makes the sphere of the Divine Sonship. It is in this knowledge that he came to know the sacred Being who rules heaven and earth as Father, as *his* Father. The consciousness which he possessed of being *the Son of God* is, therefore, nothing but the practical consequence of knowing God as the Father and as his Father. Rightly understood, the name of Son means nothing but the knowledge of God. Here, however, two observations are to be made: Jesus is convinced that he knows God in a way in which no one ever knew Him before, and he knows that it is his vocation to communicate this knowledge of God to others by word and by deed—and with it the knowledge that men are God's children. In this consciousness he knows himself to be the Son called and instituted of God, to be *the* Son of God, and hence he can say: *My* God and *my* Father, and into this invocation he puts something which belongs to no one but himself. How he came to this consciousness of the unique character of his relation to God as a Son; how he came to the consciousness of his power, and to the consciousness of the obligation and the mission which this power carries with it, is his secret, and no psychology will ever fathom it. The confidence with which John makes him address the Father: "Thou lovedst me before the foundation of the world," is undoubtedly the direct reflection of the certainty with which Jesus himself spoke. No research can carry us further. We are not even able to say when it was that he first knew himself as the Son, and whether he at once completely identified himself with this idea and let his individuality be absorbed in it, or whether it formed an inner problem which kept him in constant suspense. Only a man who had had a similar experience himself could do anything to fathom this mystery. Let a prophet try, if he chooses, to raise the veil, but, for our part, we must be content with the fact that this Jesus who preached humility and knowledge of self nevertheless named himself and himself alone as *the Son of God*. He is certain that he knows the Father, that he is to bring this knowledge to all men, and that thereby he is doing the work of God. Among all the works of God this is the greatest; it is the aim and end of all creation. The work is given to him to do, and in God's strength he will accomplish it. It was out of this feeling of power and in the prospect of victory that he uttered the words: "The Father hath committed all things unto me." Again and again in the history of mankind men of God have come forward in the sure consciousness of possessing a divine message, and of being compelled, whether they will or not, to deliver it. But the message has always happened to be imperfect; in this spot or that, defective; bound up with political or particularistic elements; designed to meet the circumstances of the moment;

and very often the prophet did not stand the test of being himself an example of his message. But in this case the message brought was of the profoundest and most comprehensive character; it went to the very root of mankind and, although set in the framework of the Jewish nation, it addressed itself to the whole of humanity—the message from God the Father. Defective it is not, and its real kernel may be readily freed from the inevitable husk of contemporary form. Antiquated it is not, and in life and strength it still triumphs to-day over all the past. He who delivered it has as yet yielded his place to no man, and to human life he still to-day gives a meaning and an aim —he *the Son of God*.

This already brings us to the other designation which Jesus gave of himself : *the Messiah*. Before I attempt briefly to explain it, I ought to mention that some scholars of note—and among them Wellhausen—have expressed a doubt whether Jesus described himself as the Messiah. In that doubt I cannot concur; nay, I think that it is only by wrenching what the evangelists tell us off its hinges that the opinion can be maintained. The very expression "Son of Man"—that Jesus used it is beyond question—seems to me to be intelligible only in a Messianic sense. To say nothing of anything else, such a story as that of Christ's entry into Jerusalem would have to be simply expunged, if the theory is to be maintained that he did not consider himself the promised Messiah and also desire to be accepted as such. Moreover, the forms in which Jesus expressed what he felt about his own consciousness and his vocation become quite incomprehensible unless they are taken as the outcome of the Messianic idea. Finally, the positive arguments which are advanced in support of the theory are either so very weak, or else so highly questionable, that we may remain quite sure that Jesus called himself the Messiah.

The idea of a Messiah and the Messianic notions generally, as they existed in Jesus' day, had been developed on two combined lines—on the line of the kings and on that of the prophets. Alien influences had also been at work, and the whole idea was transfigured by the ancient expectation that God Himself in visible form would take up the government of His people. The leading features of the Messianic idea were taken from the Israelitish kingdom in the ideal splendour in which it was invested after the kingdom itself had disappeared. Memories of Moses and of the great prophets also played a part in it. In the following lecture we shall briefly show what shapes the Messianic hopes had assumed up to Jesus' time, and in what way he took them up and transformed them.

LECTURE EIGHT

ALTHOUGH THE Messianic doctrines prevalent in the Jewish nation in Jesus' day were not a positive "dogma," and had no connexion with the legal ordinances which had been so rigidly elaborated, they formed an essential element of the hopes, religious and political, which the nation entertained for the future. They were of no very definite character, except in certain fundamental features; beyond these the greatest differences prevailed. The old prophets had looked forward to a glorious future in which God would Himself come down, destroy the enemies of Israel, and work justice, peace, and joy. At the same time, however, they had also promised that a wise and mighty king of the House of David would appear and bring this glorious state of things to pass. They had ended by indicating the people of Israel itself as the Son of God, chosen from amongst the nations of the world. These three points came to be the standard by which the Messianic ideas were subsequently elaborated. The hope of a glorious future for the people of Israel remained the frame into which all expectations were fitted, but in the two centuries before Christ the following factors were added: (i) The extension of their historical horizon strengthened the interest of the Jews in the nations of the world, introduced the notion of "mankind" as a whole and brought it within the sphere of the expected end, including, therefore, the operations of the Messiah. The day of judgment is regarded as extending to the whole world, and the Messiah not only as judging the world but as ruling it as well. (ii) Although the moral purification of the people had already been thought of earlier in connexion with the glorious future, the destruction of Israel's enemies seemed to be the main consideration; now, however, the feeling of moral responsibility and the knowledge of God as the Holy One became more active; the view comes

to prevail that the Messianic age demands a holy people, and
that the judgment must therefore of necessity also be a judgment upon a part of Israel itself. (iii) As individualism became
a stronger force, so the relation of God to the individual was
prominently emphasised. The individual Israelite comes to feel
that he is in the midst of his people, and he begins to look upon
it as a sum of individuals; the individual belief in Providence
appears side by side with the political belief, and combines with
the feeling of personal worth and responsibility; and in connexion with the expectation of the end we get the first dawn of
the hope of an eternal life and the fear of eternal punishment.
The products of this inner development are an interest in
personal salvation and a belief in the resurrection, and the
roused conscience is no longer able to hope for a glorious future
for all in view of the open profanity of the people and the
power of sin; only a remnant will be saved. (iv) The expectations for the future become more and more transcendent; they
are increasingly shifted to the realm of the supernatural and
the supramundane; something quite new comes down from
heaven to earth, and the new course on which the world enters
severs it from the old; nay, this earth, transfigured as it will be,
is no longer the final goal; the idea of an absolute bliss arises,
whose abode can only be heaven itself. (v) The personality of
the long-expected Messiah is sharply distinguished, as well from
the idea of an earthly king as from the idea of the people as
a whole, and from the idea of God. Although he appears as
a man amongst men, the Messiah retains scarcely any Messianic
traits. He is represented as with God from the first beginnings
of time; he comes down from heaven, and accomplishes his work
by superhuman means; the moral traits in the picture formed
of him come into prominence; he is the perfectly just man who
fulfils all the commandments. Nay, the idea that others benefit
by his merits forces its way in. The notion, however, of a suffering Messiah, which might seem to be suggested by Isaiah liii.,
is not reached.

But none of these speculations succeeded in displacing the
older and simpler conceptions, or in banishing that original,
patriotic, and political interpretation of them with which the

great majority of the people were familiar. God Himself assuming the sceptre, destroying His enemies, founding the Israelitish kingdom of the world, and availing Himself of a Kingly champion for the purpose; every man sitting under his own fig-tree, in his own vineyard, enjoying the fruits of peace, with his foot upon the neck of his enemies—that, after all, was still the most popular conception of the coming of the Messiah, and it was fixed in the minds even of those who were at the same time attracted to higher views. But a portion of the people had undoubtedly awakened to the feeling that the kingdom of God presupposes a moral condition of a corresponding character, and that it could come only to righteous people. Some looked to acquiring this righteousness by means of a punctilious observance of the law, and no zeal that they could show for it was enough; others, under the influences of a deeper self-knowledge, began to have a dim idea that the righteousness which they so ardently desired could itself come only from the hand of God, and that in order to shake off the burden of sin—for they had begun to be tortured by an inner sense of it—divine assistance, and divine grace and mercy, were needful.

Thus in Christ's time there was a surging chaos of opposite feelings, as well as of contradictory theories, in regard to this one matter. At no other time, perhaps, in the history of religion, and in no other people, were the most extreme antitheses so closely associated under the binding influence of religion. At one moment the horizon seems as narrow as the circle of the hills which surround Jerusalem; at another it embraces all mankind. Here everything is put upon a high plane and regarded from the spiritual and moral point of view; and there, at but a stone's throw, the whole drama seems as though it must close with a political victory for the nation. In one group all the forces of divine trust and confidence are disengaged, and the devout man struggles through to a solemn "Nevertheless"; in another, every religious impulse is stifled by a patriotic but morally obtuse fanaticism.

The idea which was formed of the Messiah must have been as contradictory as the hopes to which it was meant to respond. Not only were people's formal notions about him continually

changing—questions were being raised, for instance, as to the
sort of bodily nature which he would have—above all, his inmost character and the work to which he was to be called
appeared in diverse lights. But wherever the moral and really
religious elements had begun to get the upper hand, people were
forced to abandon the image of the political and warlike ruler,
and let that of *the prophet*, which had always to some extent
helped to form the general notion about the Messiah, take its
place. That he would bring God near; that somehow or other
he would do justice; that he would deliver from the burden
of torment within—this was what was hoped of him. The story
of John the Baptist as related in our Gospels makes it clear that
there were devout men in the Jewish nation at that time who
were expecting a Messiah in this form, or at least did not absolutely reject the idea. We learn from that story that some were
disposed to take John for the Messiah. What elasticity the
Messianic ideas must have possessed, and how far, in certain
circles, they must have travelled from the form which they
originally assumed, when this very unkinglike preacher of repentance, clad in a garment of camel's hair, and with no message
but that the nation had degenerated and its day of judgment
was at hand, could be taken for the Messiah himself. And when
the Gospels go on to tell us that not a few among the people
took Jesus for the Messiah only because he taught as one with
authority, and worked miraculous cures, how fundamentally
the idea of the Messiah seems to be changed! They regarded
this saving activity, it is true, only as the beginning of his
mission; they expected that the wonder-worker would presently
throw off his disguise and "set up the kingdom"; but all that
we are concerned with here is that they were capable of
welcoming as the promised one a man whose origin and previous
life they knew, and who had as yet done nothing but preach
repentance and proclaim that the kingdom of heaven was at
hand. We shall never fathom the inward development by which
Jesus passed from the assurance that he was the Son of God to
the other assurance that he was the promised Messiah. But
when we see that the idea which others as well had formed of
the Messiah at that time had, by a slow process of change,

developed entirely new features, and had passed from a political and religious idea into a spiritual and religious one—when we see this, the problem no longer wears a character of complete isolation. That John the Baptist and the twelve disciples acknowledged Jesus to be the Messiah; that the positive estimate which they formed of his person did not lead them to reject the shape in which he appeared, but, on the contrary, was fixed in this very shape, is a proof of the flexible character of the Messianic idea at the time, and also explains how it was that Jesus could himself adopt it. "Strength is made perfect in weakness." That there is a divine strength and glory which stands in no need of earthly power and earthly splendour, nay, excludes them; that there is a majesty of holiness and love which saves and blesses those upon whom it lays hold,—this was what he knew who in spite of his lowliness called himself the Messiah, and the same must have been felt by those who recognised him as the king of Israel anointed of God.

How Jesus arrived at the consciousness of being the Messiah we cannot explain, but still there are some points connected with the question which can be established. An inner event which Jesus experienced at his baptism was in the view of the oldest tradition the foundation of his Messianic consciousness. It is not an experience which is subject to any criticism; still less are we in a position to contradict it. On the contrary, there is a strong probability that when he made his public appearance he had already settled accounts with himself. The evangelists preface their account of his public activity with a curious story of a temptation. This story assumes that he was already conscious of being the Son of God and the one who was entrusted with the all-important work of God's people, and that he had overcome the temptations which this consciousness brought with it. When John sent to him from prison to ask: "Art thou he that should come, or do we look for another?" the answer which he sent necessarily led his questioner to understand that he was the Messiah, but *at the same time showed him how Jesus conceived the Messianic office.* Then came the day at Cæsarea Philippi, when Peter acknowledged him as the expected Messiah, and Jesus joyfully confirmed what he said.

This was followed by the question to the Pharisees, "What think ye of Christ; whose son is he?"—the scene which ended with the fresh question: "If David then call him Lord, how is he his son?" Lastly, there was the entry into Jerusalem before the whole people, together with the cleansing of the temple; actions which were equivalent to a public declaration that he was the Messiah. But his first unequivocal Messianic action was also his last. It was followed by the crown of thorns and the cross.

I have said that it is probable that when Jesus made his public appearance he had already settled accounts with himself, and was therefore clear about his mission as well. By this, however, I do not mean that, so far as he himself was concerned, he had nothing more to learn in the course of it. Not only had he to learn to suffer, and to look forward to the cross with confidence in God, but the consciousness of his Sonship was now for the first time to be brought to the test. The knowledge of the "work" which the Father had entrusted to him could not be developed except by labour and by victory over all opposition. What a moment it must have been for him when he recognised that he was the one of whom the prophets had spoken; when he saw the whole history of his nation from Abraham and Moses downwards in the light of his own mission; when he could no longer avoid the conviction that he was the promised Messiah! No longer avoid it;—for how can we refuse to believe that at first he must have felt this knowledge to be a terrible burden? Yet in saying this we have gone too far; and there is nothing more that we can say. But in this connexion we can understand that the evangelist John was right in making Jesus testify over and over again: "I have not spoken of myself, but the Father which sent me; he gave me a commandment, what I should say, and what I should speak." And again: "For I am not alone, but I and the Father that sent me."

But however we may conceive the "Messiah," it was an assumption that was simply necessary if the man who felt the inward call was to gain an absolute recognition within the lines of Jewish religious history—the profoundest and maturest history that any nation ever possessed, nay, as the future was to show, the true religious history for all mankind. The idea for the Messiah became the means—in the first instance for the devout of his own nation—of effectively setting the man who knew that he was the Son of God, and was doing the work of God, on the throne of history. But when it had accomplished this, its mission was exhausted. Jesus was the "Messiah," and was not the Messiah; and he was not the Messiah, because he left the idea far behind him; because he put a meaning into it which was too much for it to bear. Although the idea may strike us as strange we can still feel some of its meaning;—an idea which captivated a whole nation for centuries, and in which it deposited all its ideals, cannot be quite unintelligible. In the prospect of a Messianic period we see once more the old hope of a golden age; the hope which, when moralised, must necessarily be the goal of every vigorous movement in human life and forms an inalienable element in the religious view of history; in the expectation of a personal Messiah we see an expression of the fact that it is *persons* who form the saving element in history, and that if a union of mankind is ever to come about by their deepest forces and highest aims being brought into accord, this same mankind must agree to acknowledge *one* lord and master. But beyond this there is no other meaning and no other value to be attached to the Messianic idea; Jesus himself deprived it of them.

With the recognition of Jesus as the Messiah the closest possible connexion was established, for every devout Jew, between Jesus' message and his person; for it is in the Messiah's activity that God himself comes to His people, and the Messiah who does God's work and sits at the right hand of God in the clouds of heaven has a right to be worshipped. But what attitude did Jesus himself take up towards his Gospel? Does he assume a position in it? To this question there are two answers; one negative and one positive.

In those leading features of it which we described in the earlier lectures the whole of the Gospel is contained, and we must keep it free from the intrusion of any alien element: God and the soul, the soul and its God. There was no doubt in

Jesus' mind that God could be found, and had been found, in
the law and the prophets. "He hath showed thee, O man, what
is good; and what doth the Lord require of thee, but to do
justly, and to love mercy, and to walk humbly with thy God?"
He takes the publican in the temple, the widow and her mite,
the lost son, as his examples; none of them know anything
about "Christology," and yet by his humility the publican was
justified. These are facts which cannot be turned and twisted
without doing violence to the grandeur and simplicity of Jesus'
message in one of its most important aspects. To contend that
Jesus meant his whole message to be taken provisionally, and
everything in it to receive a different interpretation after his
death and resurrection, nay, parts of it to be put aside as of no
account, is a desperate supposition. No! his message is simpler
than the Churches would like to think it; simpler, but for that
very reason sterner and endowed with a greater claim to
universality. A man cannot evade it by the subterfuge of saying
that as he can make nothing of this "Christology" the message
is not for him. Jesus directed men's attention to great questions;
he promised them God's grace and mercy; he required them
to decide whether they would have God or Mammon, an eternal
or an earthly life, the soul or the body, humility or self-right-
eousness, love or selfishness, the truth or a lie. These questions
embrace the whole sphere of existence; the individual is called
upon to listen to the glad message of mercy and the Fatherhood
of God, and to make up his mind whether he will be on God's
side and the Eternal's, or on the side of the world and of time.
*The Gospel, as Jesus proclaimed it, has to do with the Father
only and not with the Son.* This is no paradox, nor, on the other
hand, is it "rationalism," but the simple expression of the actual
fact as the evangelists give it.

But no one has ever yet known the Father in the way in
which Jesus knows Him, and this knowledge of Him he brings
to other men, and thereby does "the many" an incomparable
service. He leads them to God, not only by what he says, but
still more by what he is and does, and ultimately by what he
suffers. It was in this sense that he spoke the words, "Come
unto me, all ye that labour and are heavy laden, and I will

give you rest"; as also, "The Son of man came not to be minis-
tered unto but to minister and to give his life a ransom for
many." He knows that through him a new epoch is beginning,
in which, by their knowledge of God, the "least" shall be
greater than the greatest of the ages before; he knows that in
him thousands—the very individuals who are weary and heavy
laden—will find the Father and gain life; he knows that he is
the sower who is scattering good seed; his is the field, his the
seed, his the fruit. These things involve no dogmatic doctrines;
still less any transformation of the Gospel itself, or any oppress-
ive demands upon our faith. They are the expression of an
actual fact which he perceives to be already happening, and
which, with prophetic assurance, he beholds in advance. When
under the terrible burden of his calling and in the midst of the
struggle, he comes to see that it is through him that the blind
see, the lame walk, the deaf hear, the poor have the Gospel
preached to them, he begins to comprehend the glory which
the Father has given him, and he sees that what he now suffers
in his person will, through his life crowned in death, remain a
fact efficacious and of critical importance for all time : *He is
the way to the Father, and as he is the appointed of the Father,
so he is the judge as well.*

Was he mistaken? Neither his immediate posterity, nor the
course of subsequent history, has decided against him. It is not
as a mere factor that he is connected with the Gospel; *he was
its personal realisation and its strength, and this he is felt to
be still.* Fire is kindled only by fire; personal life only by personal forces. Let us rid ourselves of all dogmatic sophistry
and leave others to pass verdicts of exclusion. The Gospel nowhere says that God's mercy is limited to Jesus' mission. But
history shows us that he is the one who brings the weary and
heavy laden to God; and, again, that he it was who raised
mankind to the new level; and his teaching is still the touchstone,
in that it brings men to bliss and brings them to judgment.

The sentence "I am the Son of God" was not inserted in the
Gospel by Jesus himself, and to put that sentence there side by
side with the others is to make an addition to the Gospel. But no
one who accepts the Gospel, and tries to understand him who

gave it to us, can fail to affirm that here the divine appeared in
as pure a form as it can appear on earth, or to feel that for those
who followed him Jesus was himself the strength of the Gospel.
What they experienced, however, and came to know in and
through him, they have told the world, and their message is
still a living force.

(6) *The Gospel and doctrine, or the question of creed*

We need not dwell long on this question, as on the essential
points everything that it is necessary to say has already been said
in the course of our previous observations.

The Gospel is no theoretical system of doctrine or philosophy
of the universe; it is doctrine only in so far as it proclaims the
reality of God the Father. It is a glad message assuring us of
life eternal, and telling us what the things and the forces with
which we have to do are worth. By treating of life eternal it
teaches us how to lead our lives aright. It tells us of the value of
the human soul, of humility, of mercy, of purity, of the cross,
and of the worthlessness of worldly goods and anxiety for the
things of which earthly life consists; and it gives the assurance
that in spite of all the struggle, peace, certainty, and something
within that can never be destroyed, will be the crown of a life
rightly led. What else can "the confession of a creed" mean
under these conditions but to do the will of God, in the certainty
that He is the Father and the one who will recompense? Jesus
never spoke of any other kind of "creed" Even when he says:
"Whosoever shall confess me before men, him will I confess
also before my Father which is in heaven," he is thinking of
people *doing as he did*; he means the confession which shows
itself in feeling and action. How great a departure from what
he thought and enjoined is involved in putting a "Christological" creed in the forefront of the Gospel, and in teaching
that before a man can approach it he must learn to think rightly
about Christ. That is putting the cart before the horse. A man
can think and teach rightly about Christ only if, and in so far
as, he has already begun to live according to Christ's Gospel.
There is no forecourt to his message through which a man

must pass; no yoke which he must first of all take upon himself. The thoughts and assurances which the Gospel provides are the first thing and the last thing, and every soul is directly arraigned before them.

Still less, however, does the Gospel presuppose any definite knowledge of nature, or stand in any connexion with such knowledge; not even in a negative sense can this contention be maintained. It is religion and the moral element that are concerned. The Gospel puts the living God before us. Here, too, the confession of Him in belief in Him and in the fulfilment of His will is the sole thing to be confessed; this is what Jesus Christ meant. So far as the knowledge is concerned—and it is vast— which may be based upon this belief, it always varies with the measure of a man's inner development and subjective intelligence. But to possess the Lord of heaven and earth as a Father is an experience which nothing else approaches; and it is an experience which the poorest soul can have, and to the reality of which he can bear testimony.

An experience—it is only the religion which a man has himself experienced that is to be confessed; every other creed or confession is in Jesus' view hypocritical and fatal. If there is no broad "theory of religion" to be found in the Gospel, still less is there any direction that a man is to begin by accepting and confessing any ready-made theory. Faith and creed are to proceed and grow up out of the all-important act of turning from the world and to God, and creed is to be nothing but faith reduced to practice. "All men have not faith," says the apostle Paul, but all men ought to be veracious and be on their guard in religion against lip-service and light-hearted assent to creeds. "A certain man had two sons; and he came to the first and said, Son, go work to-day in my vineyard. He answered and said, I will not; but afterwards he repented and went. And he came to the second, and said likewise. And he answered and said, I go, sir; and went not."

I might stop here, but I am impelled to answer one more objection. The Gospel, it is said, is a great and sublime thing, and it has certainly been a saving power in history, but it is indissolubly connected with an antiquated view of the world and history; and, therefore, although it be painful to say so, and we have nothing better to put in its place, it has lost its validity and can have no further significance for us. In view of this objection there are two things which I would like to say :

Firstly, no doubt it is true that the view of the world and history with which the Gospel is connected is quite different from ours, and that view we cannot recall to life, and would not if we could; but "indissoluble" the connexion is not. I have tried to show what the essential elements in the Gospel are, and these elements are "timeless." Not only are they so; but the man to whom the Gospel addresses itself is also "timeless," that is, it addresses itself to *man*, who, in spite of all progress and development, never changes in his inmost constitution and in his fundamental relations with the external world. Since that is so, this Gospel remains in force, then, for us too.

Secondly, the Gospel is based—and this is the all-important element in the view which it takes of the world and history— upon the antithesis between Spirit and flesh, God and the world, good and evil. Now, in spite of ardent efforts, thinkers have not yet succeeded in elaborating on a monastic basis any theory of ethics that is satisfactory and answers to the deepest needs of man. Nor will they succeed. In the end, then, it is essentially a matter of indifference what name we give to the opposition with which every man of ethical feeling is concerned : God and the world, the Here and the Beyond, the visible and the invisible, matter and spirit, the life of impulse and the life of freedom, physics and ethics. That there is a unity underlying this opposition is a conviction which can be gained *by experience*; the one realm can be subordinated to the other; but it is only by a struggle that this unity can be attained, and when it is attained it takes the form of a problem that is infinite and only approximately soluble. It cannot be attained by any refinement of a mechanical process. It is by self-conquest that a man is freed from the tyranny of matter—

Von der Gewalt die alle Wesen bindet
Befreit der Mensch sich der sich überwindet.

This saying of Goethe's excellently expressed the truth that is here in question. It is a truth which holds good for all time, and it forms the essential element in the dramatic pictures of contemporary life in which the Gospel exhibits the antithesis that is to be overcome. I do not know how our increased knowledge of nature is to hinder us from bearing witness to the truth of the creed that "The world passeth away, and the lust thereof, but he that doeth the will of God abideth for ever." We have to do with a dualism which arose we know not how; but as moral beings we are convinced that, as it has been given us in order that we may overcome it in ourselves and bring it to a unity, so also it goes back to an original unity, and will at last find its reconciliation in the great far-off event, the realised dominion of the Good.

Dreams, it may be said; for what we see before our eye is something very different. No! not dreams—after all it is here that our true life has its root—but patchwork certainly, for we are unable to bring our knowledge in space and time, together with the contents of our inner life, into the unity of a philosophic theory of the world. It is only in the peace of God which passeth all understanding that this unity dawns upon us.

But we have already passed beyond the limits of our immediate task. We proposed to acquaint ourselves with the Gospel in its fundamental features and in its most important bearings. I have tried to respond to this task; but the last point which we touched takes us beyond it. We now return to it, in order to follow, in the second part of these lectures, the course of the Christian religion through history.

LECTURE NINE

THE TASK before us in the second half of these lectures is to exhibit the history of Christian religion in its leading phases, and to examine its development in the apostolic age, in Catholicism, and in Protestantism.

THE CHRISTIAN RELIGION IN THE APOSTOLIC AGE

The inner circle of the disciples, the band of twelve whom Jesus had gathered around him, formed itself into a community. He himself founded no community in the sense of an organised union for divine worship—he was only the teacher, and the disciples were the pupils; but the fact that the band of pupils at once underwent this transformation became the ground upon which all subsequent developments rested. What were the characteristic features of this society? Unless I am mistaken, there were three factors at work in it: (i) The recognition of Jesus as the living *Lord*; (ii) the fact that in every individual member of the new community—including the very slaves— religion was *an actual experience*, and involved the consciousness of a living union with God; (iii) the leading of a *holy life* in purity and brotherly fellowship, and the expectation of the *Christ's return in the near future*.

By keeping these three factors in view we can grasp the distinctive character of the new community. Let us look at them more closely.

1. *Jesus Christ the Lord:* in thus confessing their belief in him his disciples took the first step in continuing their recognition of him as the authoritative teacher, of his word as their permanent standard of life, of their desire to keep "everything that he commanded them." But this does not express the full meaning attaching to the words "the Lord"; nay, it is far from

touching their peculiar significance. The primitive community called Jesus its Lord because he had sacrificed his life for it, and because its members were convinced that he had been raised from the dead and was then sitting on the right hand of God. There is no historical fact more certain than that the apostle Paul was not, as we might perhaps expect, the first to emphasise so prominently the significance of Christ's death and resurrection, but that in recognising their meaning he stood exactly on the same ground as the primitive community. "I delivered unto you first of all," he wrote to the Corinthians, "that which I also received, how that Christ died for our sins according to the Scriptures, and that he was buried, and that he rose again the third day." Paul did, it is true, make Christ's death and resurrection the subject of a particular speculative idea, and, so to speak, reduced the whole of the Gospel to these events; but they were already accepted as fundamental facts by the circle of Jesus' personal disciples and by the primitive community. In these two facts it may be said that the permanent recognition of Jesus Christ, and the reverence and adoration which he received, obtained their first hold. They formed the ground on which the whole Christological theory rested. But within two generations from his death Jesus Christ was already put upon the highest plane upon which men can put him. As men were conscious of him as the living Lord, he was glorified as the one who had been raised to the right hand of God and had vanquished death, as the Prince of Life, as the strength of a new existence, as the way, the truth, and the life. The Messianic ideas permitted of his being placed upon God's throne, without endangering monotheism. But, above all, he was felt to be the active principle of individual life; "it is not I that live, but Christ that liveth in me"; he is "my" life, and to press onwards to him through death is great gain. Where can we find in the history of mankind any similar instance of men eating and drinking with their master, seeing him in the characteristic aspects of his humanity, and then proclaiming him not only as the great prophet and revealer of God, but as the divine disposer of history, as the "beginning" of God's creation, and as the inner strength of a new life? It was not thus that

Mahommed's disciples spoke of their prophet. Neither is it sufficient to assert that the Messianic predicates were simply transferred to Jesus, and that everything may be explained by Jesus' expected return in glory throwing its radiance backwards. True, in the certain hope of Jesus' return, his "coming in lowliness" was overlooked; but that it was possible to conceive this certain hope and hold it fast; that in spite of suffering and death it was possible to see in him the promised Messiah; and that in and side by side with the vulgar Messianic image of him, men felt and opened their hearts to him as the present Lord and Saviour, that is what is so astonishing! It was just the death "for our sins" and the resurrection that confirmed the impression given by his person, and provided faith with a sure hold: he died as a sacrifice for us and he now lives.

There are many to-day who have come to regard both these positions as very strange, and their attitude towards them is one of indifference—towards the death, on the ground that no such significance can be attributed to a single event of this kind; towards the resurrection, because what is here affirmed to have happened is incredible.

It is not our business to defend either the view which was taken of the death, or the idea that he had risen again; but it is certainly the historian's duty to make himself so fully acquainted with both positions as to be sensible of the significance which they possessed and still possess. That these positions were of capital importance for the primitive community has never been doubted; even Strauss did not dispute it; and the great critic Ferdinand Christian Baur acknowledged that it was on the belief in them that the earliest Christian communion was built up. It must be possible, then, for us in our turn to get a feeling and an understanding for what they were; nay, perhaps we may do more; for when we probe the history of religion to the bottom, we find the truth and justice of ideas which on the surface seem so paradoxical and incredible lying at the very roots of the faith.

Let us first consider the idea that Jesus' death on the cross was one of expiation. Now, if we were to consider the conception

attaching to the words "expiatory death" in the alien realm
of formal speculation, we should, it is true, soon find ourselves
in a blind alley, and every chance of our understanding the
idea would vanish. We should be absolutely at the end of our
tether if we were to indulge in speculations as to the necessity
which can have compelled God to require such a sacrificial
death. Here, however, let us bear in mind a fact in the history
of religion which is quite universal. Those who looked upon
this death as a sacrifice soon ceased to offer God any blood-
sacrifice at all. The value attaching to such sacrifices had, it is
true, been in doubt for generations, and had been steadily
diminishing; but it was only now that the sacrifices disappeared
altogether. They did not disappear immediately or at one stroke—
this is a point with which we need not concern ourselves here
—but their disappearance took place within a very brief period
and was not delayed until after the destruction of the temple.
Further, wherever the Christian message subsequently penetrated the sacrificial altars were deserted and dealers in
sacrificial beasts found no more purchasers. If there is one thing
that is certain in the history of religion, it is that the death of
Christ put an end to all blood-sacrifices. But that they are based
on a deep religious idea is proved by the extent to which they
existed among so many nations, and they are to be judged, not
from the point of view of cold and blind rationalism, but from
that of vivid emotion. If it is obvious that they respond to a
religious need; if, further, it is certain that the instinct which
led to them found its satisfaction and therefore its goal in
Christ's death; if, lastly, there was the express declaration,
as we read in the Epistle to the Hebrews, that "by one offering
he hath perfected for ever them that are sanctified," we can
no longer feel this idea of Christ's sacrifice to be so very strange;
for history has decided in its favour, and we are beginning to
get in touch with it. His death had the value of an expiatory
sacrifice, for otherwise it would not have had strength to penetrate into that inner world in which the blood sacrifices
originated; but it was not a sacrifice in the same sense as the
others, or else it could not have put an end to them; it suppressed them by settling accounts with them. Nay, we may

go further; the validity of all material sacrifices was destroyed by Christ's death. Wherever individual Christians or whole Churches have returned to them, it has been a relapse : the earliest Christians knew that the whole sacrificial system was thenceforth abolished, and if they were asked for a reason, they pointed to Christ's death.

In the second place : any one who will look into history will find that the sufferings of the pure and the just are its saving element; that is to say, that it is not words, but deeds, and not deeds only but self-sacrificing deeds, and not only self-sacrificing deeds, but the surrender of life itself, that forms the turning-point in every great advance in history. In this sense I believe that, however far we may stand from any *theories* about vicarious sacrifice, there are few of us after all who will mistake the truth and inner justice of such a description as we read in Isa. liii. : "Surely he hath borne our griefs and carried our sorrows." "Greater love hath no man than this, that a man lay down his life for his friends"—it is in this light that Jesus' death was regarded from the beginning. Wherever any great deed has been accomplished in history, the finer a man's moral feelings are, the more sensible will he be of vicarious suffering; the more he will bring that suffering into relation to himself. Did Luther in the monastery strive only for himself?—was it not for us all that he inwardly bled when he fought with the religion that was handed down to him? But it was by the cross of Jesus Christ that mankind gained such an experience of the power of purity and love true to death that they can never forget it, and that it signifies a new epoch in their history.

Finally, in the third place : no reflection of the "reason," no deliberation of the "intelligence," will ever be able to expunge from the moral ideas of mankind the conviction that injustice and sin deserve to be punished, and that everywhere that the just man suffers, an atonement is made which puts us to shame and purifies us. It is a conviction which is impenetrable, for it comes out of those depths in which we feel ourselves to be a unity, and out of the world which lies behind the world of phenomena. Mocked and denied as though it had long perished, this truth is indestructibly preserved in the moral experience of mankind. These are the ideas which from the beginning onwards have been roused by Christ's death, and have, as it were, played around it. Other ideas have been disengaged— ideas of less importance, yet, nevertheless, very efficacious at times—but these are the most powerful. They have taken shape in the firm conviction that by his death in suffering he did a definitive work; that he did it "for us." Were we to attempt to measure and register what he did, as was soon attempted, we should fall into dreadful paradoxes; but we can in our turn feel it for ourselves with the same freedom with which it was originally felt. If we also consider that Jesus himself described his death as a service which he was rendering to many, and that by a solemn act he instituted a lasting remembrance of it—I see no reason to doubt the fact—we can understand how this death and the shame of the cross were bound to take the central place.

Jesus, however, was proclaimed as "the Lord," not only because he had died for sinners but because he was the risen and the living one. If the resurrection meant nothing but that a deceased body of flesh and blood came to life again, we should make short work of this tradition. But it is not so. The New Testament itself distinguishes between the Easter message of the empty grave and the appearances of Jesus on the one side, and the Easter faith on the other. Although the greatest value is attached to that message, we are to hold the Easter faith even in its absence. The story of Thomas is told for the exclusive purpose of impressing upon us that we must hold the Easter faith even without the Easter message: "Blessed are they that have not seen and yet have believed." The disciples on the road to Emmaus were blamed for not believing in the resurrection even though the Easter message had not yet reached them. The Lord is a Spirit, says Paul; and this carries with it the certainty of his resurrection. The Easter *message* tells us of that wonderful event in Joseph of Arimathæa's garden, which however, no eye saw; it tells us of the empty grave into which

a few women and disciples looked; of the appearance of the
Lord in a transfigured form—so glorified that his own could not
immediately recognise him; it soon begins to tell us, too, of what
the risen one said and did. The reports became more and more
complete, and more and more confident. But the Easter *faith*
is the conviction that the crucified one gained a victory over
death; that God is just and powerful; that he who is the first-
born among many brethren still lives. Paul based his Easter
faith upon the certainty that "the second Adam" was from
heaven, and upon his experience, on the way to Damascus, of
God revealing His Son to him as still alive. God, he said, revealed him "in me"; but this inner revelation was coupled with
"a vision" overwhelming as vision never was afterwards. Did
the apostle know of the message about the empty grave? While
there are theologians of note who doubt it, I think it probable;
but we cannot be quite certain about it. Certain it is that what
he and the disciples regarded as all-important was not the state
in which the grave was found, but Christ's appearances. But
who of us can maintain that a clear account of these appearances can be constructed out of the stories told by Paul and
the evangelists; and if that be impossible, and there is no
tradition of single events which is quite trustworthy, how is the
Easter faith to be based on them? Either we must decide to
rest our belief on a foundation unstable and always exposed to
fresh doubts, or else we must abandon this foundation altogether, and with it the miraculous appeal to our senses. But
here, too, the images of the faith have their roots in truth
and reality. Whatever may have happened at the grave
and in the matter of the appearances, one thing is certain:
*This grave was the birthplace of the indestructible belief that
death is vanquished, that there is a life eternal.* It is useless to
cite Plato; it is useless to point to the Persian religion, and
the ideas and the literature of later Judaism. All this would
have perished and has perished; but the certainty of the resurrection and of a life eternal which is bound up with the grave
in Joseph's garden has not perished, and on the conviction that
Jesus lives we still base those hopes of citizenship in an Eternal

City which make our earthly life worth living and tolerable. "He delivered them who through fear of death were all their lifetime subject to bondage," as the writer of the Epistle to the Hebrews confesses. That is the point. And although there be exceptions to its sway, wherever, despite all the weight of nature, there is a strong faith in the infinite value of the soul; wherever death has lost its terrors; wherever the sufferings of the present are measured against a future of glory, this feeling of life is bound up with the conviction that Jesus Christ has passed through death, that God has awakened him and raised him to life and glory. What else can we believe but that the earliest disciples also found the ultimate foundation of their faith in the living Lord to be the strength which had gone out from him? It was a life never to be destroyed which they felt to be going out from him; only for a brief span of time could his death stagger them; the strength of the Lord prevailed over everything; God did not give him over to death; he lives as the first-fruits of those who have fallen asleep. It is not by any speculative ideas of philosophy but by the vision of Jesus' life and death and by the feeling of his imperishable union with God that mankind, so far as it believes in these things, has attained to that certainty of eternal life for which it was meant, and which it dimly discerns—eternal life in time and beyond time. This feeling first established faith in the value of personal life. But of every attempt to demonstrate the certainty of "immortality" by logical process, we may say in the words of the poet :

> *Believe and venture: as for pledges,*
> *The Gods give none.*

Belief in the living Lord and in a life eternal is the *act* of the freedom which is born of God.

As the crucified and risen one Jesus was the Lord. While this confession of belief in him expressed a man's whole relation to him, it also afforded endless matter for thought and speculation. This conception of the "Lord" came to embrace the many-sided image of the Messiah and all the Old Testament prophecies of a similar kind. But as yet no ecclesiastical "doctrines" about him had been elaborated; everyone who acknowledged him as the Lord belonged to the community.

2. *Religion as an actual experience.* The second characteristic feature of the primitive community is that every individual in it, even the very slaves, possess a living experience of God. This is sufficiently remarkable; for at first sight we might think that all this devotion to Christ, and this unconditional reverence for him, must necessarily have resulted in all religion becoming a punctilious subjection to his words, and so a kind of voluntary servitude. But the Pauline epistles and the Acts of the Apostles give us quite a different picture. While they do, indeed, attest the fact that Jesus' words were held in unqualified reverence, this fact is not the most prominent feature in the picture of earliest Christendom. What is much more characteristic is that individual Christians, moved by the Spirit of God, are placed in a living and entirely personal relation to God Himself. Dr. Weinel has lately presented us with a fine book on the *Workings of the Spirit and the Spirits in the Post-apostolic Age.* It contains many passages which take us back to the apostolic age and treat in greater detail of the matters which Professor Gunkel has so impressively placed before us in his treatise on *The Holy Ghost.* The neglected problems of the extent to which, and the forms in which, the Spirit exercised an influence on the life of the early Christians, and of the view to be taken of the phenomena connected with this influence, are admirably discussed by Dr. Weinel. In substance, his conclusion is that the expressions "receiving" and "acting by" the Holy Ghost signify such an independence and immediacy of religious life and feeling, and such an inner union with God, perceived to be the mightiest reality, as could not have been expected from strict subjection to Jesus' authority. To be the child of God and to be gifted with the Spirit are simply the same as being a disciple of Christ. That a man is not truly a disciple unless he is pervaded by God's Spirit is a point which the Acts of the Apostles fully recognises. The pouring out of the Holy Spirit is placed in the forefront of the narrative. The author is conscious that the Christian religion would not be the highest and the ultimate

religion, unless it brought every individual into an immediate
and living connexion with God. This mutual union of a full
obedient subjection to the Lord with freedom in the Spirit is
the most important feature in the distinctive character of this
religion and the seal of its greatness. The workings of the Spirit
were shown everywhere, in the entire domain of the five senses,
in the sphere of will and action, in profound philosophical
speculation, and in the most delicate appreciation of the facts
of the moral life. The elementary forces of the religious tem-
perament, long held in check by systems of doctrine and the
ceremonies of public worship, were again set free. They showed
themselves in ecstatic phenomena, in signs and wonders, in an
enhancement of all the functions of life, down to conditions of
a pathological and suspicious character. The fact, however, was
not forgotten—and where it threatened to be obscured it was
strongly impressed on people's attention—that those strange
and violent phenomena were individual, but that side by side
with them there are workings of the Spirit which are bestowed
upon every one and with which no one can dispense. But "The
fruit of the Spirit," as the apostle Paul writes, "is love, joy,
peace, longsuffering, gentleness, goodness, faith, meekness,
temperance." The other feature in the distinctive character
and greatness of this religion is that it does not overestimate
the elementary strength which gave it birth; that it makes its
spiritual purport and its discipline triumph over all states of
ecstasy; and that it holds immovably to its conviction that
the Spirit of God, however it may reveal itself, is a Spirit of
holiness and of love. But here we have already passed to the
third feature which characterises early Christendom.

3. The third feature is the leading of a *holy life* in purity
and brotherly fellowship and in the expectation of Christ's
speedy return. The course which the history of the Church
followed resulted in the dogmatic details in the New Testament
being selected for investigation, rather than those parts of it
which depicted the life of the first Christians and exhorted men
to morality. And yet not only are the New Testament epistles
largely taken up with these moral exhortations, but not a few

of the so-called dogmatic portions were also written solely for moral admonition. Jesus directed his disciples to give these exhortations the first place, and the earliest Christians were well aware that the first business of life was to do the will of God and present themselves as a holy community. Upon this their whole existence and their mission in the world were based. There were two points which, in accordance with Jesus' teaching, they put first and foremost, and they were points which at bottom embraced the whole range of moral action : *purity* and *brotherly fellowship*. They took purity in the deepest and most comprehensive sense of the word, as the horror of everything that is unholy, and as the inner pleasure in everything that is upright and true, lovely and of good report. They also meant purity in regard to the body: "Know ye not that your body is the temple of the Holy Ghost which is in you? therefore glorify God in your body." In this sublime consciousness the earliest Christians took up the struggle against the sins of impurity, which in the heathen world were not accounted sins at all. As sons of God, "blameless and harmless in the midst of a crooked and perverse nation," they were to "shine as lights in the world." It was thus that they were to show of what they were made, and it was thus that they showed it : to be holy as God was holy, to be pure as disciples of Christ. Here, too, we get the measure of renunciation of the world which this community imposed upon itself. "To keep oneself unspotted from the world" was the asceticism which it practised itself and required of its adherents. The other point is *brotherly fellowship*. In joining the love of God with the love of neighbour in his sayings, Jesus himself had a new union of men with one another in view. The earliest Christians understood him. From the very first they constituted themselves into a brotherly union, not in word only but in deed—a living realisation of what he meant. In calling themselves "brothers," they felt all the obligations which the name imposes and tried to come up to them, not by legal regulations but by voluntary service, each according to the measure of his own powers and gifts. The Acts of the Apostles tell us that in Jerusalem they went so far as to have a voluntary community of goods. Paul says nothing about it; and if we are to accept this obscure report as really trustworthy, then neither Paul nor the Christian communities among the Gentiles took pattern by the enterprise. They seem not to have been required, nor to have thought it desirable, to order their lives afresh *in externals*. The brotherly fellowship which "the holy" were to cultivate, and did cultivate, was distinguished by two principles: "Whether one member suffer, all the members suffer with it," and "Bear ye one another's burdens and so fulfil the law of Christ."

LECTURE TEN

IT WAS as their Lord that the primitive community of Christians believed in Jesus. They thus expressed their absolute devotion to and confidence in him as the Prince of Life. As every individual Christian stood in an immediate relation to God through the Spirit, priests and mediations were no longer wanted. Finally, these "holy" people were drawn together into societies, which bound themselves to a strictly moral life in purity and brotherly fellowship. On the last point let me add a few words.

It is a proof of the inwardness and moral power of the new message that in spite of the enthusiasm arising from personal experience of religion, there were relatively seldom any extravagant outbursts and violent movements to be combated. Such movements may have been more frequent than the direct declarations of our authorities allow us to suppose, but they did not form the rule; and when they arose Paul was certainly not the only one who was concerned to put them down. He had certainly no wish to quench the "Spirit," but when enthusiasm threatened to lead to a repugnance to work, as in Thessalonica, or when, as in Corinth, there was a superabundance of ecstatic talk, he uttered some sober warnings: "If any would not work, neither should he eat," and "I had rather speak five words with my understanding, that by my voice I might teach others also, than ten thousand words in an unknown tongue." Still more plainly are the concentrated repose and power of the leaders shown in the moral admonitions, such as we get not only in the Pauline epistles but also, for example, in the first epistle of Peter and in the general epistle of James. Christian character is to show itself in the essential circumstances of human life, and that life is to be invigorated, supported and illumined by the Spirit. In the relation of husband to wife and of wife to

husband, of parents to childern, of masters to servants; further, in the individual's relation to constituted authority, to the surrounding heathen world, and, again, to the widow and the orphan, is "the service of God" to be proved and tested. Where have we another example in history of a religion coming in with such a robust supernatural consciousness, and at the same time laying the moral foundations of the earthly life of the community so firmly as this message? If a man fails to be inwardly affected by the faith proclaimed by the New Testament writers, he must certainly be stirred to the depths by the purity, the wealth, the power, and the delicacy of the moral knowledge which invests their exhortations with such incomparable value.

There is another feature of the life of the earliest Christians which also deserves notice in this connexion. They lived in the expectation of Christ's near return. This hope supplied them with an extraordinarily strong motive for disregarding earthly things and the joys and sufferings of this world. That they were mistaken in their expectations we must freely grant; but nevertheless it was a highly efficacious lever for raising them above the world, and teaching them to make little of small things and much of great things, and to distinguish between what is of time and what is of eternity. For a new and powerful religious impulse, which effects its own influence, to be associated with another factor which enhances and strengthens that influence, is what we see constantly happening in the history of religion. With every renewal of the religious experience of sin and grace since Augustine's day, what a lever has been supplied by the *idea of predestination*, and yet it is an idea which is in no way derived from that experience itself. How much enthusiasm was inspired in Cromwell's troops, and how greatly were the Puritans on both sides of the ocean strengthened by *the consciousness of adoption*, although this consciousness, too, was only an adjunct. When the religious experiences of St. Francis developed in the Middle Ages into a new form of devotion, how much assistance it received from the *doctrine of poverty*, and yet this doctrine was an independent force. The conviction which obtained in the apostolic age that the Lord had really appeared after his death on the cross may also be regarded in the same light. What we are thus taught is that the most inward of all possessions, namely, religion, does not struggle up into life free and isolated, but grows, so to speak, clothed in bark and cannot grow without it. In studying the apostolic age, however, it is important to observe that, not only in spite of the religious enthusiasm but even in spite of the intense eschatological hopes which prevailed, the task of making earthly life holy was not neglected.

The three principles which we have emphasised as contributing most to the characteristic features of primitive Christianity could also, if necessary, have been brought to bear within the framework of Judaism and in connexion with the synagogue. There, too, Jesus could have been acknowledged as the Lord, the new experience united with the ancestral religion, and the society of brothers developed in the form of a Jewish conventicle. In Palestine, as a matter of fact, this was the form which the earliest communities took. But the new principles displayed great vigour and pointed far beyond Judaism : Jesus Christ the Lord is not only Israel's Lord, but the Lord of history, the Lord of all men. The new experience of a direct union with God makes the old worship with its priests and mediations unnecessary. The society of brothers towers over all other associations and deprives them of any value. The inner development which the new tendency virtually comprised began at once. Paul was not the first to start it; before and side by side with him there were obscure and nameless Christians in the dispersion who took up Gentiles into the new society. They did away with the particularistic and statutory regulations of the law by declaring that these were to be understood in a purely spiritual sense and to be interpreted as symbols. There was a branch of the Jewish world outside Palestine where this declaration had long taken actual effect—it is true, on other grounds—and where the Jewish religion was being freed from its limitations by a process of philosophical interpretation which was bringing it to the level of a spiritual religion for the whole world. This development may be regarded in the light of a preliminary stage in the history of Christianity, and was in many respects really so. It was the stage on which these name-less Christians entered. It was the path upon which a deliver-ance from historical Judaism and its outworn religious ordinances was capable of gradual attainment. But one thing is certain; it was not the goal of the movement. So long as the words "the former religion is done away with" remained unspoken, there was always a fear that in the next generation the old regulations would be brought forward again in their literal meaning. How often and often in the history of religion has there been a ten-dency to do away with some traditional form of doctrine or ritual which has ceased to satisfy inwardly, but to do away with it by giving it a new interpretation. The endeavour seems to be succeed-ing; the temper and the knowledge prevailing at the moment are favourable to it—when, lo and behold! the old meaning suddenly comes back again. The actual words of the ritual, of the liturgy, of the official doctrine, prove stronger than anything else. If a new religious idea cannot manage to make a radical breach with the past *at the critical point*—the rest may remain as it is—and procure itself a new "body," it cannot last; it dis-appears again. There is no tougher or more conservative fabric than a properly constituted religion; it can only yield to a higher phase by being abolished. No permanent effect, then, could be expected in the apostolic age from the twisting and turning of the law so as to make room for the new faith side by side with it, or so as to approximate the old religion to that faith. Someone had to stand up and say "The old is done away with"; he had to brand any further pursuit of it as a *sin*; he had to show that all things were become new. The man who did that was the apostle Paul, and it is in having done it that his greatness in the history of the world consists.

Paul is the most luminous personality in the history of primi-tive Christianity, and yet opinions differ widely as to his true significance. Only a few years ago we had a leading Protestant theologian asserting that Paul's rabbinical theology led him to corrupt the Christian religion. Others, conversely, have called him the real founder of that religion. But in the opinion of the great majority of those who have studied him the true view is that he was the one who understood the master and continued his work. This opinion is borne out by the facts. Those who blame him for corrupting the Christian religion have never felt a single breath of his spirit, and judge him only by mere externals, such as clothes and book-learning; those who extol or criticise him as a founder of religion are forced to make him bear witness against himself on the main point, and acknowledge that the consciousness which bore him up and steeled him for his work was illusory and self-deceptive. As we cannot want to be wiser than history, which knows him only as Christ's missionary, and as his own words clearly attest what his aims were and what he was, we regard him as Christ's disciple, as the apostle who not only worked harder but also accomplished more than all the rest put together.

It was Paul who delivered the Christian religion from Judaism. We shall see how he did that if we consider the following points :

It was Paul who definitely conceived the Gospel as the message of redemption already effected and of salvation now present. He preached the crucified and risen Christ, who gave us access to God and therewith righteousness and peace.

It was he who confidently regarded the Gospel as a new force abolishing the religion of the law.

It was he who perceived that religion in its new phase pertains to the individual and therefore to all individuals; and in this conviction, and with a full consciousness of what he was doing, he carried the Gospel to the nations of the world and transferred it from Judaism to the ground occupied by Greece and Rome. Not only are Greeks and Jews to unite on the basis of the Gospel, but the Jewish dispensation itself is now at an end. That the Gospel was transplanted from the East, where in subsequent ages it was never able to thrive properly, to the West, is a fact which we owe to Paul.

It was he who placed the Gospel in the great category of spirit *versus* flesh, inner *versus* outer existence, life *versus* death; he, born a Jew and educated a Pharisee, gave it a *language*, so that it became intelligible, not only to the Greeks but to

all men generally, and united with the whole of the intellectual
capital which had been amassed in previous ages.

These are the factors that go to make the apostle's greatness
in the history of religion. On their inner connexion I cannot
here enter in any detail. But, in regard to the first of them, I
may remind you of the words of the most important historian
of religion in our day. Wellhausen declares that "Paul's especial
work was to transform the Gospel of the kingdom into the
Gospel of Jesus Christ, so that the Gospel is no longer the
prophecy of the coming of the kingdom but its actual fulfilment by Jesus Christ. In his view, accordingly, redemption
from something in the future has become something which has
already happened and is now present. He lays far more emphasis on faith than on hope; he anticipates the sense of future
bliss in the present feeling of being God's son; he vanquishes
death and already leads the new life on earth. He extols the
strength which is made perfect in weakness; the grace of God
is sufficient for him, and he knows that no power, present or
future, can take him from His love, and that all things work
together for good to them that love God." What knowledge,
what confidence, what strength, was necessary to tear the new
religion from its mother earth and plant it in an entirely new
one! Islam, originating in Arabia, has remained the Arabian
religion, no matter where it may have penetrated. Buddhism
has at all times been at its purest in India, but this religion,
born in Palestine, and confined by its founder to Jewish ground,
in only a few years after his death was severed from that connexion. Paul put it in competition with the Israelitish religion:
"Christ is the end of law." Not only did it bear being thus
rooted up and transplanted, but it showed that it was meant
to be transplanted. It gave stay and support to the Roman
empire and the whole world of Western civilisation. If, as
Renan justly observes, anyone had told the Roman emperor in
the first century that the little Jew who had come from Antioch
as a missionary was his best collaborator, and would put the
empire upon a stable basis, he would have been regarded as a
madman, and yet the statement would have been quite true.
Paul brought new forces to the Roman empire, and laid the

foundations of Western and Christian civilisation. Alexander
the Great's work has perished; Paul's has remained. But if we
praise the man who, without being able to appeal to a single
word of his master's, undertook such a bold venture by the help
of the spirit and with the letter against him, we must none the
less pay the meed of honour to those personal disciples of Jesus
who after a bitter internal struggle ultimately associated themselves with Paul's principles. That Peter did so we know for
certain; of others we hear that they at least acknowledged
their validity. It was, indeed, no insignificant circumstance
that men in whose ears every word of their master's was still
ringing, and in whose recollection the concrete features of his
personality were still a vivid memory—that these faithful disciples should recognise a pronouncement to be true which in
important points seemed to depart from the original message
and portended the downfall of the religion of Israel. What was
kernel here, and what was husk, history has itself showed with
unmistakable plainness, and by the shortest process. Husk were
the whole of the Jewish limitations attaching to Jesus' message;
husk were also such definite statements as "I am not sent but
unto the lost sheep of the house of Israel." In the strength of
Christ's spirit the disciples broke through these barriers. It was
his personal disciples—not, as we might expect, the second or
third generation, when the immediate memory of the Lord
had already paled—who stood the great test. That is the most
remarkable fact of the apostolic age.

Without doing violence to the inner and essential features
of the Gospel—unconditional trust in God as the Father of
Jesus Christ, confidence in the Lord, forgiveness of sins, certainty of eternal life, purity and brotherly fellowship—Paul
transformed it into the universal religion, and laid the ground
for the great Church. But whilst the original limitations fell
away, new ones of necessity made their appearance; and they
modified the simplicity and the power of a movement which was
from within. Before concluding our survey of the apostolic age,
we must direct attention to these modifications.

In the first place: the breach with the synagogue and the
founding of entirely independent religious communities had

well-marked results. Whilst the idea was firmly maintained that
the community of Christ, the "Church," was something supra-
sensible and heavenly, because it came from within, there was
also a conviction that the Church took visible shape in every
separate community. As a complete breach had taken place, or
no connexion been established, with the ancient communion, the
formation of entirely new societies was logically invested with a
special significance and excited the liveliest interest. In his sayings and parables Jesus, careless of all externals, could devote
himself solely to the all-important point; but *how and in what
forms* the seed would grow was not a question which occupied
his mind; he had the people of Israel with their historical
ordinances before him and was not thinking of external changes.
But the connexion with this people was now severed, and no
religious movement can remain in a *bodiless* condition. It must
elaborate *forms* for common life and common public worship.
Such forms, however, cannot be improvised; some of them take
shape slowly out of concrete necessities; others are derived from
the environment and from existing circumstances. It was in this
way that the "Gentile" communities procured themselves an
organism, a body. The forms which they developed were in part
independent and gradual, and in part based upon the facts with
which they had to deal.

But a special measure of value always attaches to forms. By
being the means by which the community is kept together, *the
value of that to which they minister is insensibly transferred to
them*; or, at least, there is always a danger of this happening.
One reason for this is that the observance of the forms can
always be controlled or enforced, as the case may be; whilst for
the inner life there is no control that cannot be evaded.

When the breach with the Jewish national communion had
once taken place, there could be no doubt about the necessity
for setting up a new community in opposition to it. The self-
consciousness and strength of the Christian movement was displayed in the creation of a Church which knew itself to be the
true Israel. But the founding of churches and "the Church" on
earth brought an entirely new interest into the field; what came
from within was joined by something that came from without;

law, discipline, regulations for ritual and doctrine, were developed, and began to assert a position by a logic of their own. The measure of value applicable to religion itself no longer remained the only measure, and with a hundred visible threads religion was insensibly worked into the net of history.

In the second place: we have already referred to the fact that it was above all in his Christology that Paul's significance as a teacher consisted. In his view—we see this as well by the way in which he illuminated the death on the cross and the resurrection, as by his equation, "the Lord is a Spirit"—the redemption is already accomplished and salvation a present power. "God hath reconciled us to Himself through Jesus Christ"; "If any man be in Christ, he is a new creature"; "Who shall separate us from the love of God?" The absolute character of the Christian religion is thus made clear. But it may also be observed in this connexion that every attempt to formulate a theory has a logic of its own and dangers of its own. There was one danger which the apostle himself had to combat, that of men claiming to be redeemed without giving practical proof of the new life. In the case of Jesus' sayings no such danger could arise, but Paul's formulas were not similarly protected. That men are not to rely upon "redemption," forgiveness of sin, and justification, if the hatred of sin and the imitation of Christ be lacking, inevitably became in subsequent ages a standing theme with all earnest teachers. Who can fail to recognise that the doctrines of "material redemption" have been the occasion of grievous temptations in the history of the Church, and for whole generations concealed the true meaning of religion? The conception of "redemption," which cannot be inserted in Jesus' teaching in this free and easy way at all, became a snare. No doubt it is true that Christianity is the religion of redemption; but the conception is a delicate one, and can never be taken out of the sphere of personal experience and inner reformation.

But here we are met by a second danger closely connected with the first. If redemption is to be traced to Christ's person and work, everything would seem to depend upon a right understanding of this person together with what he accomplished. *The formation of a correct theory of and about Christ threatens*

*to assume the position of chief importance, and to pervert the
majesty and simplicity of the Gospel.* Here, again, the danger is
of a kind such as cannot arise with Jesus' sayings. Even in John
we read: "If ye love me, keep my commandments." But with
the way in which Paul defined the theory of religion, the danger
can certainly arise and did arise. How long was it before the
Church began to teach that the all-important thing was to
know how the person of Jesus was constituted, what sort of
physical nature he had, and so on? Paul himself is far removed
from this position—"Whoso calleth Christ Lord speaketh by the
Holy Ghost"—but the way in which he ordered his religious
conceptions, as the outcome of his speculative ideas, unmistakably exercised an influence in a wrong direction. That, however great the attraction which his way of ordering them may
possess for the understanding, it is a perverse proceeding to make
Christology the fundamental substance of the Gospel, is shown
by Christ's teaching, which is everywhere directed to the all-
important point, and summarily confronts every man with his
God. This does not, however, prevent Paul from epitomising the
Gospel in the message of Christ crucified; thus exhibiting God's
power and God's wisdom, and in the love of Christ kindling the
love of God. There are thousands to-day in whom the Christian
faith is still propagated in the same manner, namely, through
Christ. But to demand assent to a series of propositions about
Christ's person is a different thing altogether.

There is, however, another point to be considered here. Under
the influence of the Messianic dogmas, and led by the impression
which Christ made, Paul became the author of the speculative
idea that not only was God in Christ, but that Christ himself
was possessed of a peculiar nature of a heavenly kind. With the
Jews, this was not a notion that necessarily shattered the framework of the Messianic idea; but with the Greeks it inevitably
set an entirely new theory in motion. Christ's *appearance* in
itself, the entrance of a divine being into the world, came of
necessity to rank as the chief fact, as itself *the real redemption.*
Paul did not, indeed, himself look upon it in this light; for him
the crucial facts are the death on the cross and the resurrection,
and he regards Christ's entrance into the world from an ethical

point of view and as an example for us to follow: "For our sakes he became poor"; he humbled himself and renounced the world. But this state of things could not last. The appearance in itself could not permanently occupy the second place; it was too large. But when moved into the first place it threatened the very existence of the Gospel, by drawing away men's thoughts and interests in another direction. When we look at the history of dogma, who can deny that that was what happened? To what extent it happened we shall see in the following lectures.

In the third place; the new Church possessed a sacred book, the Old Testament. Although Paul taught that the law had become of no avail, he found a means of preserving the whole of the Old Testament. What a blessing to the Church this book has proved! As a book of edification, of consolation, of wisdom, of counsel, as a book of history, what an incomparable importance it has had for Christian life and apologetics! Which of the religions that Christianity encountered on Greek or Roman ground could boast of a similar book? Yet the possession of this book has not been an unqualified advantage to the Church. To begin with, there are many of its pages which exhibit a religion and a morality other than Christian. No matter how determined people were to spiritualise it and give it an inner meaning by construing it in some special way, their efforts did not avail to get rid of the original sense in its entirety. There was always a danger of an inferior and obsolete principle forcing its way into Christianity through the Old Testament. This, indeed, was what actually occurred. Nor was it only in individual aspects that it occurred; the whole aim was changed. Moreover, on the new ground religion was intimately connected with a political power, namely, with nationality. How if people were seduced into again seeking such a connexion, not, indeed, with Judaism, but with a new nation, and not with ancient national laws, but with something of an analogous character? And when even a Paul here and there declared Old Testament laws to be still authoritative in spite of their having undergone an allegorical transformation, how could anyone restrain his successors from also proclaiming other laws, remodelled to suit the circumstances of the time, as valid ordinances of God? This brings us to the second point. Although whatever was drawn from the Old Testament by way of authoritative precept may have been inoffensive in substance, it was a menace to Christian freedom of both kinds. It threatened the freedom which comes from within, and also the freedom to form church communities and to arrange for public worship and discipline.

I have tried to show that the *limitations* which surrounded the Gospel did not cease with the severance of the tie binding it to Judaism, but that, on the contrary, new obstacles made their appearance. *They arose, however, just at the very points upon which the necessary progress of things depended, or, as the case might be, where an inalienable possession like the Old Testament was in question.* Here, again, then, we are reminded of the fact that, so far as history is concerned, as soon as we leave the sphere of pure inwardness, there is no progress, no achievement, no advantage of any sort, that has not its dark side, and does not bring its disadvantages with it. The apostle Paul complained that "we know in part." To a much greater degree is the same thing true of our actions and of everything connected with them. We have always to "pay the penalty" of acting, and not only take the evil consequences but also knowingly and with open eyes deliberately neglect one thing in order to gain another. Our purest and most sacred possessions, when they leave the inward realm and pass into the world of form and circumstance, are no exception to the rule that the very shape which they take in action also proves to be their limitation.

When the great apostle ended his life under Nero's axe in the year 64, he could say of himself what a short time before he had written to a faithful comrade : "I have finished my course; I have kept the faith." What missionary is there, what preacher, what man entrusted with the cure of souls, who can be compared with him, whether in the greatness of the task which he accomplished, or in the holy energy with which he carried it out? He worked with the most living of all messages; and kindled a fire; he cared for his people like a father and strove for the souls of others with all the forces of his own; at the same time he discharged the duties of the teacher, the schoolmaster, the organiser. When he sealed his work by his death, the Roman empire from Antioch as far as Rome, nay, as far as Spain, was planted with Christian communities. There were to be found in them few that were "mighty after the flesh" or of noble degree, and yet they were as "lights in the world," and on them the progress of the world's history rested. They had little "illumination," but they had acquired the faith in the living God and in a life eternal; they knew that the value of the human soul is infinite, and that its value is determined by relation to the invisible; they led a life of purity and brotherly fellowship, or at least strove after such a life. Bound together into a new people in Jesus Christ, their head, they were filled with the high consciousness that Jews and Greeks, Greeks and barbarians, would through them become one, and that the last and highest stage in the history of humanity had been reached.

LECTURE ELEVEN

THE APOSTOLIC age now lies behind us. We have seen that in the course of it the Gospel was detached from the mother-soil of Judaism and placed upon the broad field of the Græco-Roman empire. The apostle Paul was the chief agent in accomplishing this work, and in thereby giving Christianity its place in the history of the world. The new connexion which it thus received did not in itself denote any restricted activity; on the contrary, the Christian religion was intended to be realised in mankind, and mankind at that time meant the *orbis Romanus*. But the new connexion involved the development of new forms, and new forms also meant limitation and encumbrance. We shall see more closely how this was effected if we consider

THE CHRISTIAN RELIGION IN ITS DEVELOPMENT
INTO CATHOLICISM

The Gospel did not come into the world as a statutory religion, and therefore none of the forms in which it assumed intellectual and social expression—not even the earliest—can be regarded as possessing a classical and permanent character. The historian must always keep this guiding idea before him when he undertakes to trace the course of the Christian religion through the centuries from the apostolic age downwards. As Christianity rises above all antitheses of the Here and the Beyond, life and death, work in the world and holding aloof from it, reason and ecstasy, Hebraism and Hellenism, it can also exist under the most diverse conditions; just as it was originally amid the wreck of the Jewish religion that it developed its power. Not only can it so exist—it must do so, if it is to be the religion of the living and is itself to live. As a Gospel it has only *one* aim—the finding of the living God, the finding of Him by every individual

139

as *his* God, and as the source of strength and joy and peace. How this aim is progressively realised through the centuries—whether with the help of factors like Hebraism or Hellenism, holding aloof from the world or civilising it, Gnosticism or Agnosticism, ecclesiastical institution or perfectly free union, or whatever other kinds of bark there may be which protect the core and allow the sap to rise—is a matter that is of secondary moment, that is exposed to change, that belongs to the centuries, that comes with them and with them perishes.

Now the greatest transformation which the new religion ever experienced—almost greater even than that which gave rise to the Gentile Church and thrust the Palestinian communities into the background—falls in the second century of our era, and therefore in the period which we shall consider in the present lecture.

If we place ourselves at about the year 200, about a hundred or a hundred and twenty years after the apostolic age—not more than three or four generations had gone by since that age came to an end—what kind of spectacle does the Christian religion offer?

We see a great ecclesiastical and political community, and side by side with it numerous "sects" calling themselves Christian, but denied the name and bitterly opposed. That great ecclesiastical and political community presents itself as a league of individual communities spanning the Empire from end to end. Although independent they are all constituted essentially alike, and interconnected by one and the same law of doctrine, and by fixed rules for the purposes of intercommunion. The law of doctrine seems at first sight to be of small scope, but all its tenets are of the widest significance; and together they embrace a profusion of metaphysical, cosmological, and historical problems, give them definite answers, and supply particulars of mankind's developments from the creation up to its future form of existence. Jesus' injunctions for the conduct of life are not included in this law of doctrine; as the "rule of discipline" they were sharply distinguished from the "rule of faith." Each church, however, also presents itself as an institution for public worship, where God is honoured in conformity with a solemn ritual. The dis-

tinction between priests and laymen is already a well-marked
characteristic of this institution; certain acts of divine worship
can be performed only by the priest; his mediation is an absolute
necessity. It is only by mediation that a man can approach God
at all, by the mediation of right doctrine, right ordinance, and a
sacred book. The living faith seems to be transformed into a
creed to be believed; devotion to Christ, into Christology; the
ardent hope for the coming of "the kingdom," into a doctrine
of immortality and deification; prophecy, into technical exegesis
and theological learning; the ministers of the Spirit, into clerics;
and brothers, into laymen in a state of tutelage; miracles and
miraculous cures disappear altogether, or else are priestly devices;
fervent prayers become solemn hymns and litanies; the "Spirit"
becomes law and compulsion. At the same time individual
Christians are in full touch with the life of the world, and the
burning question is, "In how much of this life may I take part
without losing my position as a Christian?" This enormous
transformation took place within a hundred and twenty years.
The first thing which we have to determine is, How did that
happen? next, Did the Gospel succeed in holding its own amid
this change, and how did it do so?

Before, however, we try to answer these two questions we must
call to mind a piece of advice which no historian ought ever to
neglect. Anyone who wants to determine the real value and significance of any great phenomenon or mighty product of history
must first and foremost inquire into the work which it accomplished, or, as the case may be, into the problem which it solved.
As every individual has a right to be judged, not by this or that
virtue or defect, not by his talents or by his frailties, but by
what he has done, so the great edifices of history, the States and
the Churches, must be estimated first and foremost, we may
perhaps say, exclusively, by what they have achieved. It is *the
work done* that forms the decisive test. With any other test we
are landed in judgments of the vaguest kind, now optimistic,
now pessimistic, and mere historical twaddle. So here, too, in
considering *the Church as developed into Catholicism*, we must
first of all ask, In what did its work consist? What problem did
it solve? What did it achieve? I will answer the last question

first. It achieved two things : it waged war with nature-worship, polytheism, and political religion, and beat them back with great energy; and it exploded the dualistic philosophy of religion. Had the Church at the beginning of the third century been asked by way of reproach, "How could you so far forget your beginnings and to what have you come?" it might have answered : "Yes, I have come to this; I have been obliged to discard much and take up much; I have had to fight—my body is full of scars, and my clothes are covered with dust; but I have won my battles and built my house; I have beaten back poly-theism; I have disabled and almost annihilated that monstrous abortion, political religion; I have resisted the enticements of a subtle religious philosophy, and victoriously encountered it with God the almighty Creator of all things; lastly, I have reared a great building, a fortress with towers and bulwarks, where I guard my treasure and protect the weak." This is the answer which the Church might have given, and truthfully given. But, some one may object, it was no great achievement to wage war with nature-worship and polytheism, and to beat them back; they had already rotted and decayed, and had little strength left. The objection does not hold. Many of the forms in which that species of religion had taken shape were, no doubt, anti-quated and approaching extinction, but the religion itself, *the religion of nature*, was a mighty foe. It even still avails to beguile our souls and touch our heart-strings with effect, when an inspired prophet voices its message; how much more so then! The hymn to the Sun, giving life to all that lives, produced a profound and lifelong religious impression even upon a Goethe, and made him into a Sun-worshipper. But how overpowering it was in the days before science had banished the gods from nature. Christianity exploded the religion of nature—exploded it not for this or that individual; that was already done—but ex-ploded it in the sense that there was now a large and compact community refuting nature-worship and polytheism by its impressive doctrines, and affording the deeper religious temper stay and support. And then political religion! Behind the imperial cult there was the whole power of the State, and to come to terms with it looked so safe and easy—yet the Church did not yield a single inch; it abolished the imperial system of state-idols. It was to place an irremovable landmark between religion and politics, between God and Cæsar, that the martyrs shed their blood. Lastly, in an age that was deeply moved by questions of religious philosophy, the Church maintained a firm front against all the speculative ideas of Dualism; and, although these ideas often seemed to approximate closely to its own position, it passionately met them with the monotheistic view. Here, however, the struggle was rendered all the harder by the fact that many Christians—and just, too, the most prominent and talented—made common cause with the enemy, and themselves embraced the dualistic theory. The Church stood firm. If we recollect that, in spite of these counter-movements against the Græco-Roman spirit, it also managed to attach this very spirit of itself—otherwise than Judaism, to whose dealings with the Greek world the saying may be applied, "You had power to draw but not to hold me"; if we recollect, further, that it was in the second century that the foundations of the whole of the ecclesiastical system prevailing up to the present day were laid, we can only be astonished at the greatness of the work which was then achieved.

We now return to the two questions which we raised: How was this great transformation accomplished? and did the Gospel hold its own amid this change, or, if so, how?

There were, if I am not mistaken, three leading forces engaged in bringing about this great revolution, and effecting the formation of new forms. The first of these forces tallies with a universal law in the history of religion, for in every religious development we find it at work. When the second and third generations after the founding of a new religion have passed away; when hundreds, nay thousands, have become its adherents, no longer through conversion but by the influences of tradition and of birth—despite Tertullian's saying, *fiunt non nascuntur Christiani*; when those who have laid hold upon the faith as great spoil are joined by crowds of others who wrap it round them like an outer garment, a revolution always occurs. The religion of strong feeling and of the heart passes into the religion of custom and therefore of form and of law. A new religion may be instituted with the greatest vigour, the utmost enthusiasm, and a tremendous amount of inner emotion; it may at the same time lay ever so much stress on spiritual freedom—where was all this ever more powerfully expressed than in Paul's teaching? —and yet, even though believers be forced to be celibates and only adults be received, the process of solidifying and codifying the religion is bound to follow. Its forms then at once stiffen; in the very process of stiffening they receive for the first time a real significance, and new forms are added. Not only do they acquire the value of laws and regulations, but they come to be insensibly regarded as though they contained within them the very substance of religion; nay, as though they were themselves that substance. This is the way in which people who do not feel religion to be a reality are compelled to regard it, for otherwise they would have nothing at all; and this is the way in which those who continue really to live in it are compelled to handle it, or else they would be unable to exercise any influence upon others. The former are not by any means necessarily hypocrites. Real religion, of course, is a closed book to them; its most important element has evaporated. But there are various points of view from which a man may still be able to appreciate religion without living in it. He may appreciate it as discharging the functions of morality, or of policy; above all, he may appreciate it on æsthetic grounds. When the Romanticists re-introduced Catholicism into Germany and France at the beginning of the nineteenth century, Chateaubriand, more especially, was never tired of singing its praises, and fancied that he had all the feelings of a Catholic. But an acute critic remarked that Monsieur Chateaubriand was mistaken in his feelings; he thought that he was a true Catholic, while as a matter of fact he was only standing before the ancient ruin of the Church and exclaiming: "How beautiful!" That is one of the ways in which a man can appreciate a religion without being an inward adherent of it; but there are many others, and amongst them some in which a nearer approach is made to its true substance. All of them, however, have this much in common, that any actual experience of religion is no longer felt, or felt only in an uncertain and intermittent

way. Conversely, a high regard is paid to the outward shows
and influences connected with it, and they are carefully maintained. Whatever finds expression in doctrines, regulations,
ordinances and forms of public worship comes to be treated as the
thing itself. This, then, is the first force at work in the transformation : *the original enthusiasm*, in the large sense of the
word, *evaporates*, and the religion of law and form at once
arises.

But not only did an original element evaporate in the course
of the second century; another was introduced. Even had this
youthful religion not severed the tie which bound it to Judaism,
it would have been inevitably affected by the spirit and the
civilisation of that Græco-Roman world on whose soil it was
permanently settled. But to what a much greater extent was it
exposed to the influence of this spirit after being sharply severed
from the Jewish religion and the Jewish nation. It hovered
bodiless over the earth like a being of the air; bodiless and seeking
a body. The spirit, no doubt, makes to itself its own body, but
it does so by assimilating what is around it. *The influx of Hellenism, of the Greek spirit,* and the union of the Gospel with it,
form the greatest fact in the history of the Church in the second
century, and when the fact was once established as a foundation
it continued through the following centuries. In the influence of
Hellenism on the Christian religion three stages may be distinguished, and a preliminary stage as well. We have already
mentioned the preliminary stage in a previous lecture. It is to
be found in the circumstances in which the Gospel arose, and it
formed a very condition of its appearance. Not until Alexander
the Great had erected an entirely new position of affairs, and
the barriers separating the nations of the East from one another
and from Hellenism had been destroyed, could Judaism free
itself from its limitations and start upon its development into a
religion for the world. The time was ripe when a man in the
East could also breathe the air of Greece and see his spiritual
horizon stretch beyond the limits of his own nation. Yet we cannot say that the earliest Christian writings, let alone the Gospel,
show, to any considerable extent, the presence of a Greek element.
If we are to look for it anywhere—apart from certain well-marked

traces of it in Paul, Luke, and John—it must be in the *possibility* of the new religion appearing at all. We cannot enter further upon this question here. The first stage of any real influx of definitely Greek thought and Greek life is to be fixed at about the year 130. It was then that the religious philosophy of Greece began to effect an entrance, and it went straight to the centre of the new religion. It sought to get into inner touch with Christianity, and, conversely, Christianity itself held out a hand to this ally. We are speaking of Greek *philosophy*; as yet, there is no trace of mythology, Greek worship, and so on; all that was taken up into the Church, cautiously and under proper safe-guards, was the great capital which philosophy had amassed since the days of Socrates. A century or so later, about the year 220 or 230, the second stage begins; Greek mysteries, and Greek civilisation in the whole range of its development, exercise their influence on the Church, but not mythology and polytheism; these were still to come. Another century, however, has in its turn to elapse before Hellenism as a whole and in every phase of its development was established in the Church. Safeguards, of course, are not lacking here either, but for the most part they consist only in a change of label; the thing itself is taken over without alteration, and in the worship of the saints we see a regular Christian religion of a lower order arising. We are here concerned, however, not with the second and third stage, but only with that influx of the Greek spirit which was marked by the absorption of Greek philosophy and, particularly, of Platonism. Who can deny that elements here came together which stood in elective affinity? So much depth and delicacy of feeling, so much earnestness and dignity, and—above all—so strong a *monotheistic* piety were displayed in the religious ethics of the Greeks, acquired as it had been by hard toil on a basis of inner experience and metaphysical speculation, that the Christian religion could not pass this treasure by with indifference. There was much in it, indeed, which was defective and repellent; there was no personality visibly embodying its ethics as a living power; it still kept up a strange connexion with "demon-worship" and polytheism; but both as a whole and in its individual parts it was felt to contain a kindred element, and it was absorbed.

But besides the Greek ethics there was also a cosmological conception which the Church took over at this time, and which was destined in a few decades to attain a commanding position in its doctrinal system—*the Logos*. Starting from an examination of the world and the life within, Greek thought had arrived at the conception of an *active central idea*—by what stages we need not here mention. This central idea represented the unity of the supreme principle of the world, of thought, and of ethics; but it also represented, at the same time, the divinity itself as a creative and active as distinguished from a quiescent power. The most important step that was ever taken in the domain of Christian doctrine was when the Christian apologists at the beginning of the second century drew the equation: the Logos = Jesus Christ. Ancient teachers before them had also called Christ "the Logos" among the many predicates which they assigned to him; nay, one of them, John, had already formulated the proposition, "The Logos is Jesus Christ." But with John this proposition had not become the basis of every speculative idea about Christ; with him, too, "the Logos" was only a predicate. But now teachers came forward who previous to their conversion had been adherents of the Platonico-stoical philosophy, and with whom the conception "Logos" formed an inalienable part of a general philosophy of the world. They proclaimed that Jesus Christ was the Logos incarnate, which had hitherto been revealed only in the great effects which it exercised. In the place of the entirely unintelligible conception "Messiah," an intelligible one was acquired at a stroke; Christology, tottering under the exuberance of its own affirmations, received a stable basis; Christ's significance for the world was established; his mysterious relation to God was explained; the cosmos, reason, and ethics, were comprehended as one. It was, indeed, a marvellous formula; and was not the way prepared for it, nay hastened, by the speculative ideas about the Messiah propounded by Paul and other ancient teachers? The knowledge that the divine in Christ must be conceived as the Logos opened up a number of problems, and at the same time set them definite limits and gave them definite directives. Christ's unique character as opposed to all rivals appeared to be established in the simplest fashion, and yet the conception provided thought with so much liberty and free play that Christ could be regarded, as the need might arise, on the one side as operative deity itself, and on the other as still the first-born among many brethren and as *the first created* of God.

What a proof it is of the impression which Christ's teaching created that Greek philosophers managed to identify him with the Logos! For the assertion that the incarnation of the Logos had taken place in a historical personage there had been no preparation. No philosophising Jew had ever thought of identifying the Messiah with the Logos; no Philo, for instance, ever entertained the idea of such an equation! *It gave a metaphysical significance to a historical fact; it drew into the domain of cosmology and religious philosophy a person who had appeared in time and space*; but by so distinguishing one person it raised all history to the plane of the cosmical movement.

The identification of the Logos with Christ was the determining factor in the fusion of Greek philosophy with the apostolic inheritance, and led the more thoughtful Greeks to adopt the latter. Most of us regard this identification as inadmissible, because the way in which we conceive the world and ethics does not point to the existence of any Logos at all. But a man must be blind not to see that for that age the appropriate formula for uniting the Christian religion with Greek thought was the Logos. Nor is it difficult even to-day to attach a valid meaning to the conception. An unmixed blessing it has not been. To a much larger extent than the earlier speculative ideas about Christ it absorbed men's interest; it withdrew their minds from the simplicity of the Gospel, and increasingly transformed it into a philosophy of religion. The proposition that the Logos had appeared among men had an intoxicating effect, but the enthusiasm and transport which it produced in the soul did not lead with any certainty to the God whom Jesus Christ proclaimed.

The loss of an original element and the gain of a fresh one, namely, the Greek, are insufficient to explain the great change which the Christian religion experienced in the second century. We must bear in mind, thirdly, the great struggle which that religion was then carrying on within its own domain. Parallel with the slow influx of the element of Greek philosophy experiments were being made all along the line in the direction of what may be briefly called "acute Hellenisation." While they offer us a most magnificent historical spectacle, in the period itself they were a terrible danger. More than any before it, the second century is the century of religion fusion, of "Theocrasia." The problem was to include Christianity in this religious fusion, as one element among others, although the chief. The "Hellenism" which made this endeavour had already attracted to itself all the mysteries, all the philosophy of Eastern worship, elements the most sublime and the most absurd, and by the never-failing aid of philosophical, that is to say, of allegorical interpretation, had spun them all into a glittering web. It now fell upon—I cannot help so expressing it—the Christian religion. It was impressed by the sublime character of this religion; it did reverence to Jesus Christ as the Saviour of the world; it offered to give up everything that it possessed—all the treasures of its civilisation and its wisdom—to this message, if only the message would suffer them to stand. As though endowed with the right to rule, the message was to make its entry into a ready-made theory of the world and religion and into mysteries already prepared for it. What a proof of the impression which this message made, and what a temptation! This "Gnosticism"—such is the name which the movement has received—strong and active in the abundance of its religious experiments, established itself under Christ's name, developed a vigorous and abiding feeling for many Christian ideas, sought to give shape to what was still shapeless, to settle accounts with what was externally incomplete, and to bring the whole stream of the Christian movement into its own channel. The majority of the faithful, led by their bishops, so far from yielding to these enticements, took up the struggle with them in the conviction that they masked a demoniac temptation. But struggle in this case meant definition, that is to say, drawing a sharp line of demarcation around what was Christian and declaring everything heathen that would not keep within it. *The struggle with Gnosticism compelled the Church to put its teaching, its worship, and its discipline, into fixed forms and ordinances, and to exclude everyone who would not yield them*

obedience. In the conviction that it was everywhere only con-
serving and honouring what had been handed down, it never for
a moment doubted that the obedience which it demanded was
anything more than subjection to the divine will itself, and that
in the doctrines with which it encountered the enemy it was
exhibiting *the impress of religion itself.*

If by "Catholic" we mean the Church of doctrine and of
law, then the Catholic Church had its origin in the struggle
with Gnosticism. It had to pay a heavy price for the victory which
kept that tendency at bay; we may almost say that the vanquished imposed their terms upon the victor: *Victi victoribus
legem dederunt.* It kept Dualism and the acute phase of Hellenism at bay; but by becoming a community with a fully worked
out scheme of doctrine, and a definite form of public worship,
it was of necessity compelled to take on forms analogous to those
which it combated in the Gnostic. To encounter our enemy's
theses by setting up others one by one, is to change over to his
ground. How much of its original freedom the Church sacrificed!
It was now forced to say: You are no Christian, you cannot
come into any relation with God at all, unless you have first of
all acknowledged these doctrines, yielded obedience to these
ordinances, and sought out definite forms of mediation. Nor
was anyone to think a religious experience legitimate that had
not been sanctioned by sound doctrine and approved by the
priests. The Church found no other way and no other means
of maintaining itself against Gnosticism, and what was set up
as a protection against enemies from without became the
palladium, nay, the very foundation, within. This entire development, it is true, would probably have taken place apart from the
struggle in question—the two elements which we first discussed
would have produced it—but that it took place so rapidly and
assumed so positive, nay, so Draconian, a shape, was due to the
fact that the struggle was one in which the very existence of the
traditional religion was at stake. The superficial view that the
personal ambition of certain individuals was at the bottom of
the whole system of established ordinance and priesthood is
absolutely untenable. The loss of the original, living element is
by itself sufficient to explain the phenomena. *La médiocrité*

fonde l'autorité. It is the man who knows religion only as usage and obedience that creates the priest, for the purpose of ridding himself of an essential part of the obligations which he feels by loading him with them. He also makes ordinances, for the semi-religious prefer an ordinance to a Gospel.

We have endeavoured to indicate the tendencies by which the great change was effected. It remains to answer the second question : Did the Gospel hold its own amid the change, and, if so, how? That it entered upon an entirely new set of circumstances is already obvious; we shall, however, have to study them more closely.

LECTURE TWELVE

No one can compare the internal state of Christendom at the beginning of the third century with the state in which it found itself a hundred and twenty years earlier without being moved by conflicting views and sentiments. Admiration for the vigorous achievement presented in the creation of the Catholic Church, and for the energy with which it extended its activity in all directions, is balanced by concern at the absence of those many elements of freedom and directness, united, however, by an inward bond, which the primitive age possessed. Although we are compelled gratefully to acknowledge that this Church repelled all attempts to let the Christian religion simply dissolve into contemporary thought, and protected itself against the acute phase of Hellenisation, still we cannot shut our eyes to the fact that it had to pay a high price for maintaining its position. Let us determine a little more precisely what the alteration was which was effected in it, and on which we have already touched.

The first and most prominent change is the way in which freedom and independence in matters of religion is endangered. No one is to feel and count himself a Christian, that is to say, a child of God, who has not previously subjected his religious knowledge and experience to the controlling influence of the Church's creed. The "Spirit" is confined within the narrowest limits, and forbidden to work where and as it will. Nay, more; not only is the individual, except in special cases, to begin by being a minor and by obeying the Church; he is never to become of full age, that is to say, he is never to lose his dependence on doctrine, on the priest, on public worship, and on the "book." It was then that what we still specifically call the Catholic form of godliness, in contrast with the Protestant, originated. A blow was dealt at the direct and immediate element in religion; and for any individual to restore it afresh for himself became a matter of extraordinary difficulty.

Secondly, although the acute phase of Hellenisation was avoided, Christendom became more and more penetrated by the Greek and philosophical idea that true religion is first and foremost "doctrine," and doctrine, too, that is co-extensive with the whole range of knowledge. That this faith of "slaves and old women" attracted to itself the entire philosophy of God and the world which the Greeks had formed, and undertook to recast that philosophy as though it were actually of its own substance, and unite it with the teaching of Jesus Christ, was certainly a proof of the inner power of the Christian religion; but the process involved, as a necessary consequence, a displacement of the fundamental religious interest, and the addition of an enormous burden. The question, "What must I do to be saved?" which in Jesus Christ's and the apostles' day could still receive a very brief answer, now evoked a most diffuse one; and even though a shorter answer might still be provided for the laymen, they were in so far regarded as deficient, and expected to observe a submissive attitude towards the learned. The Christian religion had already received that tendency to Intellectualism which has clung to it ever since. But when thus presented as a huge and complex fabric, as a vast and difficult system of doctrine, not only is it encumbered, but its earnest character threatens to disappear. This character depends upon the emotional and gladdening element in it being kept directly accessible. The Christian religion is assuredly informed with the desire to come to terms with all knowledge and with intellectual life as a whole; but when achievements in this field—even presuming that they always accord with truth and reality—are held to be equally binding with the Gospel message, or even to be a necessary preliminary to it, mischief is done to the cause of religion. This mischief is already unmistakably present at the beginning of the third century.

Thirdly, the Church obtained a special, independent value as an *institution*; it became a *religious power*. Originally only a developed form of that community of brothers which furnished place and manner for God's common worship and a mysterious shadow of the heavenly Church, it now became, *as an institution*, an indispensable factor in religion. People were taught that in this institution Christ's Spirit had deposited everything that the individual man can need; that he is wholly bound to it, therefore, not only in love but also in faith; that it is there only that the Spirit works, and therefore there only that all its gifts of grace are to be found. That the individual Christian who did not subordinate himself to the ecclesiastical institution relapsed, as a rule, into heathenism, and fell into false and evil doctrines or an immoral life, was, indeed, an actual fact. The effect of this, combined with the struggle against the Gnostics, was that the institution, together with all its forms and arrangements, became more and more identified with the "bride of Christ," "the true Jerusalem," and so on, and accordingly was even itself proclaimed as the inviolable creation of God, and the fixed and unalterable abode of the Holy Ghost. Consistently with this, it began to announce that all its ordinances were equally sacred. How greatly religious liberty was thus encumbered I need not show.

Fourthly and lastly, the Gospel was not proclaimed as the glad message with the same vigour in the second century as it had been in the first. The reasons for this are manifold; on the one hand personal experience of religion was not felt so strongly as Paul, or as the author of the fourth Gospel, felt it; on the other, the prevalent eschatological expectations, which those teachers had restrained by their more profound teaching, remained in full sway. *Fear* and *hope* are more prominent in the Christianity of the second century than they are with Paul, and it is only in appearance that the former stands nearer to Jesus' sayings; for, as we saw, God's Fatherhood is the main article in Jesus' message. But, as Romans viii. proves, the knowledge of this truth is just what Paul embodied in his preaching of the faith. While the element of *fear* thus obtained a larger scope in the Christianity of the second century—this scope increased in proportion as the original buoyancy died down and conformity to the world extended—the ethical element became less free and more a matter of law and of rigorous insistence on small points. In religion, "rigorism" always forms the obverse side of secularity. But as it appeared impossible to expect a rigoristic ethics of every one, the distinction between a perfect and a sufficient morality already set in as an element in the growth of Catholicism. That the roots of this distinction go further back is a fact of which we need not here take account; it was only towards the end of the second century that the distinction became a fatal one. Born of necessity and erected into a virtue, it soon grew so important that the existence of Christianity as a Catholic Church came to depend upon it. The uniformity of the Christian ideal was thereby disturbed and a quantitative view of moral achievement suggested which is unknown to the Gospel. The Gospel does, no doubt, make a distinction between a strong and a weak faith, and greater and smaller moral achievements; but he that is least in the kingdom of God may be perfect in his kind.

These various tendencies together denote the essential changes which the Christian religion experienced up to the beginning of the third century, and by which it was modified. Did the Gospel hold its own in spite of them, and how may that be shown? Well, we can cite a whole series of documents, which, so far as written words can attest inner and genuinely Christian life, bear very clear and impressive testimony that such life existed. Martyrdoms like those of Perpetua and Felicitas, or letters passing between communities, like those from Lyons to Asia Minor, exhibit the Christian faith and the strength and delicacy of moral sentiment with a splendour only paralleled in the days when the faith was founded; while of all that had been done in the external development of the Church they make no mention whatever. The way to God is found with certainty, and the simplicity of the life within does not appear to be disturbed or encumbered. Again, let us take a writer like the Christian religious philosopher, Clement of Alexandria, who flourished about the year 200. We can still feel from his writings that this scholar, although he was absolutely steeped in speculative ideas, and as a thinker reduced the Christian religion to a boundless sea of "doctrines"—a Greek in every fibre of his being—won peace and joy from the Gospel. He can also express what he won and testify of the power of the living God. It is as a new man that he appears, one who has pressed on through the whole range of philosophy, through authority and speculation, through all the externals of religion, to the glorious liberty of the children of God. His faith in Providence, his faith in Christ, his doctrine of freedom, his ethics—everything is expressed in language that betrays the Greek, and yet everything is new and genuinely Christian. Further, if we compare him with a Christian of quite another stamp, namely, his contemporary Tertullian, it is easy to show that *what they have in common in religion is what they have learned from the Gospel, nay, is the Gospel itself.* And in reading and studying Tertullian's exposition of the Lord's Prayer we see that this hot-blooded African, this stern foe of heretics, this resolute champion of *auctoritas* and *ratio*, this dogmatic advocate, this writer at once Churchman and enthusiast, nevertheless possessed a deep feeling for the main substance of the Gospel and a good knowledge of it as well. In this Old-Catholic Church the Gospel, truly, was not as yet stifled!

Further, this Church still kept up the all-important idea that the Christian community must present itself as a society of brothers active in work, and it gave expression to this idea in a way that puts subsequent generations to shame.

Lastly, there can be no doubt—and while so truth-loving a man as Origen confirms the fact for us, heathen writers like Lucian also attest it—that the hope of an eternal life, the full confidence in Christ, a readiness to make sacrifices, and a purity of morals, were still, in spite of all frailties—here, too, not lacking —the *real* characteristics of this society. Origen can challenge his heathen opponents to compare any community whatever with the Christian community, and to say where the greater moral excellence lies. This religion had, no doubt, already developed a husk and a covering; to penetrate through to it and grasp the kernel had become more difficult; it had also lost much of its original life. But the gifts and the tasks which the Gospel offered still remained in force, and the fabric which the Church had erected around them also served many a man as the means by which he attained to the thing itself.

We now pass to the consideration of

THE CHRISTIAN RELIGION IN GREEK CATHOLICISM

I must invite you to descend several centuries with me and to look at *the Greek Church* as it is to-day, and as it has been preserved, essentially unaltered, for more than a thousand years. Between the third and the nineteenth century the history of the Eastern Church nowhere presents any great breach, and therefore we may permissibly take up our position in the present. Here, in turn, we ask the three following questions:

What did this Greek Catholicism achieve?

What are its characteristics?

What modifications did the Gospel here undergo, and how did it hold its own?

What did this Greek Catholicism achieve? On this point two facts may be cited : firstly, in the great domain which it embraces, the countries of the Eastern part of the Mediterranean and northwards to the Arctic Ocean, it made an end of heathenism and polytheism. The decisive victory was achieved from the third to the sixth century, and so effectually achieved that the gods of Greece really perished—perished unwept and unmourned. They died, not in any great battle, but from sheer exhaustion, and without offering any resistance worth mention. I may just point out that before dying they transferred a considerable portion of their power to the Church's saints. But, what is more important, with the death of the gods, Neoplatonism, the last great product of Greek philosophy, was also vanquished. The religious philosophy of the Church proved the stronger. The victory over Hellenism is an achievement of the Eastern Church on which it still subsists. Secondly, this Church managed to effect such a fusion with the individual nations which it drew into its bosom that religion and church became to them national palladia, nay, palladia pure and simple. Go amongst Greeks, Russians, Armenians, etc., and you will everywhere find that religion and nationality are inseparable, and the one element exists only in and alongside of the other. Men of these nationalities will, if need be, suffer themselves to be cut in pieces for their religion. This is no mere consequence of the pressure exercised by the hostile power of Mohammedanism;

the Russians are not subject to this pressure. Nor is it only—shall I say?—in the Moscow press that we can see what a firm and intimate connexion exists between Church and nation in these peoples, in spite of "sects" which are not wanting here either; to convince ourselves of it we must read—to take an instance at random—Tolstoi's *Village Tales*. They bring before the reader a really touching picture of the deep influence of the Church with its message of the Eternal, of self-sacrifice, of sympathy and fraternity, on the national mind. That the clergy stand low in the social scale, and frequently encounter contempt, must not delude us into supposing that as the representatives of the Church they do not occupy an incomparably high position. In Eastern Europe the monastic ideal is deeply rooted in the national soul.

But the mention of these two points includes everything that can be said about the achievements of this Church. To add that it has disseminated a certain amount of culture would involve pitching our standard of culture very low. In comparison with Islam, too, it is no longer so successful in doing what it has done in the past and still does in regard to polytheism. The missions of the Russian Church are still overthrowing polytheism even to-day; but large territories have been lost to Islam, and the Church has not recovered them. Islam has extended its victories as far as the Adriatic and in the direction of Bosnia. It has won over numerous Albanian and Slav tribes which were once Christian. It shows itself to be at least a match for its rival, although we must not forget that in the heart of its dominions there are Christian nations who have maintained their creed.

Our second question was, What are the characteristics of this Church? The answer is not easy; for as it presents itself to the spectator this Church is a highly complex structure. The feelings, the superstitions, the learning, and the devotional philosophy of hundreds, nay, of thousands of years, are built into it. But, further; no one can look at this Church from outside, with its forms of worship, its solemn ritual, the number of its ceremonies, its relics, pictures, priests, monks, and the philosophy of its mysteries, and then compare it on the one hand with the Church of the first century and on the other with the Hellenic cults in the

age of Neoplatonism, without arriving at the conclusion that it
belongs not to the former but to the latter. *It takes the form,
not of a Christian product in Greek dress, but of a Greek product
in Christian dress.* It would have done battle with the Christians
of the first century just as it did battle with the worship of Magna
Mater and Zeus Soter. There are innumerable features of this
Church which are counted as sacred as the Gospel, and towards
which not even a tendency existed in primitive Christianity.
The same thing may be said in the main of the whole perform-
ance of its chief religious service, nay, even of many of its
dogmas : if certain words, like Christ, etc., are omitted, there is
nothing left to recall the original element. *In its external form
as a whole* this Church is nothing more than a *continuation of
the history of Greek religion* under the alien influence of
Christianity, parallel to the many other alien influences which
have affected it. We might also describe it as the natural product
of the union between Hellenism, itself already in a state of
Oriental decay, and Christian teaching; it is the transformation
which history effects in a religion by "natural" means, and, as
was here the case, was bound to effect between the third and
the sixth century. In this sense it is a *natural religion.* The conception admits of a double meaning. It is generally understood
as an abstract term covering all the elementary feelings and
processes traceable in every religion. Whether there are any
such elements, or, on the other hand, whether they are sufficiently
stable and articulate to be followed as a whole, admits, however,
of a doubt. The conception "natural religion" may be better
applied to the final product of a religion as arising when the
"natural" forces of history have ceased playing on it. At bottom
these forces are everywhere the same, although differing in the
way in which they are displayed. They mould religion until it
answers their purpose; not by expelling what is sacred, venerable,
and so on, but by assigning it the place and allowing it the scope
which they consider right. They immerse everything in a uniform
medium—that medium which, like the air, is the first condition
of their "natural" existence. In this sense, then, the Greek Church
is a *natural* religion; no prophet, no reformer, no genius, has
arisen in its history since the third century to disturb the ordinary

process by which a religion becomes naturalised into common history. The process attained its completion in the sixth century and asserted itself victoriously against heavy assaults in the eighth and ninth. The Church has since been at rest, and no further essential, nay, not even any unessential, change has taken place in the condition which it then reached. Since then, apparently, the nations belonging to this Church have encountered nothing to make it seem intolerable to them and to call for any reform in it. They still continue, then, in this "natural" religion of the sixth century.

I have, however, advisedly spoken of the Church *in* its *external form*. That we cannot arrive at its inner condition by simple deduction from its outer is part of its complex character. It is not sufficient to observe, then, although the observation is correct, that this Church fits into the history of Greek religion. It also produces effects which from this point of view are not easily intelligible. We cannot form a correct estimate of it unless we dwell more closely on the factors which lend it its character.

The first factor which we encounter is *tradition* and its observance. The sacred and the divine do not exist in a state in which they can act freely—we shall see later to what reservations this statement is subject—but are put, as it were, into a storehouse, in the form of an immense capital. The capital is to provide for all demands, and to be coined in the precise way in which the Fathers coined it. Here, it is true, we have an idea which can be traced to something already existing in the primitive age. We read in the Acts of the Apostles that "They continued steadfastly in the apostles' doctrine," but what became of this discipline and the obligation to follow it? Firstly, everything was designated "apostolic" which was deposited in this Church during the succeeding centuries; or, rather, what the Church felt itself bound to possess in order to adapt itself to the historical position in which it was placed, it called apostolic, because it fancied that otherwise it could not exist, and so it argued that what is necessary for the Church's existence *must* be apostolic. Secondly, it has been established as an irrefragable fact that the "continuing steadfastly in the apostles' doctrine" applies, first and foremost, to the punctilious observance of all ritual ordinances : the sacred element is bound up with *text* and *form*. Both are conceived in a thoroughly antique way. That the divine is, so to speak, stored up as though it were an actual commodity, and that the supreme demand which the Deity makes is the punctilious observance of a ritual, were ideas that in antiquity were perfectly familiar and admitted of no doubt. Tradition and ceremony are the conditions under which the Holy alone existed and was accessible. Obedience, respect, reverence, were the most important religious feelings. Whilst they are doubtless inalienable features of religion, it is only as accompaniments of an active feeling quite different in its character that they possess any value; and this further presumes that the object to which they are directed is a worthy one. Traditionalism and the ritualism so closely connected with it are prominent characteristics of the Greek Church, but this is just what shows how far it has departed from the Gospel.

The second point that fixes the character of this Church is the value which it attaches to *orthodoxy*, to sound doctrine. It has stated and re-stated its doctrines with the greatest precision and often enough made them a terror to men of a different creed. No one, it claims, can be saved who does not possess the correct doctrine; the man who does not possess it is to be expelled and must forfeit all his rights; if he be a fellow-countryman, he must be treated as a leper and lose all connexion with his nation. This fanaticism, which still flares up here and there in the Greek Church even to-day and in principle has not been abandoned, is not Greek, although a certain inclination towards it was not lacking in the ancient Greeks; still less did it originate in Roman law; it is the result, rather, of an unfortunate combination of several factors. When the Roman empire became Christian, the hard fight for existence which the Church had waged with the Gnostics was not yet forgotten; still less had the Church forgotten the last bloody persecutions which the State had inflicted upon it in a kind of despair. These two circumstances would in themselves be sufficient to explain how the Church came to feel that it had a right of reprisal, and was at the same time bound to suppress heretics. But, in addition, there had now appeared in the highest place, since the days of Diocletian and Constantine, the absolutist conception, derived from the East, of the unlimited right and the unlimited duty of the ruler in regard to his "subjects." The unfortunate factor in the great change was that the Roman emperor was at once, and almost in the same moment, a Christian emperor and an Oriental despot. The more conscientious he was, the more intolerant he was bound to be; for the Deity had committed to his care not only men's bodies but their souls as well. Thus arose the aggressive and all-devouring orthodoxy of State and Church, or, rather, of the State-Church. Examples always to hand from the Old Testament completed and sanctified the process.

Intolerance was a new growth in the land of the Greeks, and cannot be roundly laid to their charge; but the way in which doctrine developed, namely, as a philosophy of God and the world, was due to their influence; and the fact that religion and doctrine were directly identified is also a product of the Greek spirit. No mere reference to the significance which doctrine already possessed in the apostolic age, and to the tendencies operating in the direction of bringing it into a speculative form, is sufficient to explain the change. These are points, rather, as I hope that I have shown in the previous lectures, which bear a different interpretation. It is in the second century, and with the apologists, that Intellectualism commences; and, supported by the struggle with the Gnostics and by the Alexandrian school of religious philosophers in the Church, it managed to prevail.

But it is not enough to assess the teaching of the Greek Church by its formal side alone, and ascertain in what way and to what extent it is exhibited, and what is the value to be placed upon it. We must also examine its substance; for it possesses two features which are quite peculiar to it and separate it from the Greek philosophy of religion—*the idea of the creation*, and the doctrine of the *God-Man nature of the Saviour*. We shall treat of these two elements in our next lecture, and, further, of the two other features which, side by side with tradition and doctrine, characterise the Greek Church; namely, the form of worship and the order of monkhood.

LECTURE THIRTEEN

So far we have established the fact that Greek Catholicism is characterised as a religion by two elements : by *traditionalism* and by *intellectualism*. According to traditionalism the reverent preservation of the received inheritance, and the defence of it against all innovation, is not only an important duty, but is itself the practical proof of religion. That is an idea quite in harmony with antiquity but foreign to the Gospel; for the Gospel knows absolutely nothing of intercourse with God being bound up with reverence for tradition itself. But the second element, intellectualism, is also of Greek origin. The elaboration of the Gospel into a vast philosophy of God and the world, in which every conceivable kind of material is handled; the conviction that because Christianity is the absolute religion it must give information on all questions of metaphysics, cosmology, and history; the view of revelation as a countless multitude of doctrines and explanations, all equally holy and important—this is Greek intellectualism. According to it, *Knowledge* is the highest good, and spirit is spirit only in so far as it knows; everything of an æsthetical, ethical, and religious character must be converted into some form of knowledge, which human will and life can then follow with safety. The development of the Christian faith into an all-embracing theosophy, and the identification of faith with theological knowledge, are proofs that the Christian religion on Greek soil entered the proscribed circle of the native religious philosophy and has remained there.

But in this vast philosophy of God and the world, which possesses an absolute value as the "substance of what has been revealed" and as "orthodox doctrine," there are two elements which radically distinguish it from Greek religious philosophy and invest it with an entirely original character. I do not mean the appeal which it makes to revelation—for to that the

Neoplatonists also appealed—but the *idea of creation* and the doctrine of *the God-Man nature of the Saviour*. They traverse the scheme of Greek religious philosophy at two critical points, and have therefore always been felt to be alien and intolerable by its genuine representatives.

The idea of creation we can deal with in a few words. It is undoubtedly an element which is as important as it is in thorough keeping with the Gospel. It abolishes all interfusion of God and world, and gives expression to the power and actuality of the living God. Attempts were not wanting, it is true, among Christian thinkers on Greek soil—just because they were Greeks —to conceive the Deity only as the uniform power operating in the fabric of the world, as the unity in diversity, and as its goal. Traces of this speculative idea are even still to be found in the doctrine of the Greek Church; the idea of creation, however, triumphed, and therewith Christianity won a real victory.

The subject of the God-Man nature of the Saviour is one on which it is much more difficult to arrive at a correct opinion. It is undubitably the central point in the whole dogmatic system of the Church. It supplied the doctrine of the Trinity. In the Greek view these two doctrines together make up Christian teaching *in nuce*. When a Father of the Greek Church once said, as he did say : "The idea of the God-Man nature, the idea of God becoming a man, is what is new in the new, nay, is the only thing new under the sun," not only did he correctly represent the opinion of all his fellow-believers, but he also at the same time strikingly expressed their view that, while sound intelligence and earnest reflection yield all the other points of doctrine of themselves, this one lies beyond them. *The theologians of the Greek Church are convinced that the only real distinction between the Christian creed and natural philosophy is that the former embraces the doctrine of the God-Man nature*, including the Trinity. Side by side with this, the only other doctrine that can at most come in question is that of creation.

If that be so, it is of radical importance to obtain a correct view of the origin, meaning, and value of this doctrine. In its completed form it must look strange to anyone who comes to it straight from the evangelists. While no study of history can rid

us of the impression that the whole fabric of ecclesiastical Christology is a thing absolutely outside the concrete personality of
Jesus Christ, there are, however, historical considerations which
enable us not only to explain its origin, but also even to justify,
in a certain degree, the way in which it took shape. Let us try
to get a clear idea of the leading points.

We saw in a previous lecture how it came about that the
Church teachers selected the conception of the Logos in order
to define Christ's nature and majesty. They found the conception of the "Messiah" quite unintelligible; it conveyed no
meaning to them. As conceptions cannot be improvised, they
had to choose between representing Christ as a deified man, that
is to say, as a hero, or conceiving his nature after the pattern of
one of the Greek gods, or identifying it with the Logos. The first
two possibilities had to be put aside, as they were "heathenish,"
or seemed to be so.

There remained, therefore, the Logos. How well this formula
served different purposes we have already pointed out. Did it
not readily admit of being combined with the conception of the
Sonship, without leading to any objectional theogonies? It involved, too, no menace to monotheism. But the formula had a
logic of its own, and this logic led to results which were not
absolutely free from suspicion. The conception of the Logos was
susceptible of very varied expression; in spite of its sublime
meaning, it could be also so conceived as to permit of the bearer
of the title not being by any means of a truly divine nature but
possessing one that was only half divine.

The question as to the more exact definition of the nature of
the Logos-Christ could not have attained the enormous significance which it received in the Church, and might have been
stilled by various speculative answers, if it had not been accompanied by the triumph of a very precise idea of the nature of
redemption, which acted as a peremptory challenge. Among
all the possible ideas on the subject of redemption—forgiveness
of sins, release from the power of the demons, and so on—that
idea came victoriously to the front in the Church in the third
century which conceived of it as *redemption from death and
therewith as elevation to the divine life, that is to say, as*

deification. It is true that this conception found a safe starting-point in the Gospel, and support in the Pauline theology; but in the form in which it was now developed it was foreign to both of them and conceived on Greek lines; *mortality is in itself reckoned as the greatest evil, and as the cause of all evil, while the greatest of blessings is to live for ever.* What a severely Greek idea this is we can see, in the first place, from the fact that redemption from death is presented, in a wholly realistic fashion, as a *pharmacological* process—the divine nature has to flow in and transform the mortal nature—and, in the second, from the way in which eternal life and deification were identified. But if actual interference in the constitution of human nature and its deification are involved, then *the redeemer must himself be God and must become man.* It is only on this condition that so marvellous a process can be imagined as actually taking place. Word, doctrine, individual deeds, are here of no avail—how can life be given to a stone, or a mortal made immortal, by preaching at them? Only when the divine itself bodily enters into mortality can mortality be transformed. It is not, however, the hero, but God Himself alone, who possesses the divine, that is to say, eternal life, and so possesses it as to permit of His *giving it to others.* The Logos, then, must be God Himself, and He must have actually become man. With the satisfying of these two conditions, real, natural redemption, that is to say, the deification of humanity, is actually effected. These considerations enable us to understand the prodigious disputes over the nature of the Logos-Christ which filled several centuries. They explain why Athanasius strove for the formula that the Logos-Christ was of the same nature as the Father, as though the existence or non-existence of the Christian religion were at stake. They show clearly how it was that other teachers in the Greek Church regarded any menace to the complete *unity* of the divine and the human in the Redeemer, any notion of a merely moral connexion, as a death blow to Christianity. These teachers secured their formulas, which for them were anything but scholastic conceptions; nay, they were the statement and establishment of a matter of fact, in the absence of which the Christian religion was as unsatisfactory as any other. The doctrines of the identical

nature of the three persons of the Trinity—how the doctrine of
the Holy Ghost came about, I need not mention—and of the
God-Man nature of the Redeemer are in strict accordance with
the distinguishing notion of the redemption as a deification of
man's nature by making him immortal. Without the help of
the notion those formulas would never have been attained; but
they also stand and fall with it. They prevailed, however, not
because they were akin to the ideas of Greek philosophy, but
because they were contrasted with them. Greek philosophy never
ventured, and never aspired, to meet in any similar way by
"history" and speculative ideas that wish for immortality which
it so vividly entertained. To attribute any such interference with
the Cosmos to a *historical* personality and the manner in which
it appeared, and to ascribe to that personality a transformation
in what, given once for all, was in a state of eternal flux, must
necessarily have seemed, to Greek philosophy, pure mythology
and superstition. The "only new thing under the sun" must
necessarily have appeared to it, and did appear, to be the worst
kind of fable.

The Greek Church still entertains the conviction to-day that
in these doctrines it possesses the essence of Christianity, regarded
at once as a mystery and as a mystery that has been revealed.
Criticism of this contention is not difficult. We must acknowledge that those doctrines powerfully contributed to keeping
the Christian religion from dissolving into Greek religious
philosophy; further, that they profoundly impress us with the
absolute character of this religion; again, that they are in actual
accordance with the Greek notion of redemption; lastly, that this
very notion has *one* of its roots in the Gospel. But beyond this we
can acknowledge nothing; nay, it is to be observed (i) that the
notion of the redemption as a deification of mortal nature is
subchristian, *because the moral element involved can at best be
only tacked on to it*; (ii) that the whole doctrine is inadmissible,
because it has scarcely any connexion with the Jesus Christ of
the Gospel, and its formulas do not fit him; it is, therefore, not
founded on truth; and (iii) that as it is connected with the real
Christ only by uncertain threads, it leads us away from him;
it does not keep his image alive, but on the contrary, demands

that this image should be apprehended solely in the light of alleged hypotheses about him expressed in theoretical propositions. That this substitution produces no very serious or destructive effects is principally owing to the fact that in spite of them the Church has not suppressed the Gospels, and that their own innate power makes itself felt. It may also be conceded that the notion of God having become man does not everywhere produce the effect only of a bewildering mystery, but, on the contrary, is capable of leading to the pure and definite conviction that God was in Christ. We may admit, lastly, that the egoistic desire for immortal existence will, within the Christian sphere, experience a moral purification through the longing *to live with and in God*, and to remain inseparably bound to His love. But all these admissions cannot do away with the palpable fact that in Greek dogma we have a fatal connexion established between the desire of the ancients for immortal life and the Christian message. Nor can anyone deny that this connexion, implanted in Greek religious philosophy and the intellectualism which characterised it, has led to formulas which are incorrect, introduce a supposititious Christ in the place of the real one, and, besides, encourage the delusion that, if only a man possesses the right formula, he has the thing itself. Even though the Christological formula were the theologically right one—what a departure from the Gospel is involved in maintaining that a man can have no relation with Jesus Christ, nay, that he is sinning against him and will be cast out, unless he first of all acknowledges that Christ was *one* person with two natures and two powers of will, one of them divine and one human. Such is the demand into which intellectualism has developed. Can such a system still find a place for the Gospel story of the Syrophœnician woman or the centurion at Capernaum?

But with traditionalism and intellectualism a further element is associated, namely, ritualism. If religion is presented as a complex system of traditional doctrine, to which the few alone have any real access, the majority of believers cannot practise it at all except as ritual. *Doctrine comes to be administered in stereotyped formulas accompanied by symbolic acts.* Although no inner understanding of it is thus possible, it produces the feeling of something mysterious. The very deification which the future is expected to bring, and which in itself is something that can neither be described nor conceived, is now administered by means of ritual acts, as though it were an earnest of what is to come. An imaginative mood is excited, and disposes to its reception; and this excitement, when enhanced, is its seal.

Such are the feelings which move the members of the Greek Catholic Church. Intercourse with God is achieved through the cult of a mystery, and by means of hundreds of efficacious formulas small and great, signs, pictures, and consecrated acts, which, if punctiliously and submissively observed, communicate divine grace and prepare the Christian for eternal life. Doctrine as such is for the most part something unknown; if it appears at all, it is only in the form of liturgical aphorisms. For ninety-nine per cent. of these Christians, religion exists only as a ceremonious ritual, in which it is externalised. But even for Christians of advanced intelligence all these ritual acts are absolutely necessary, for it is only in them that doctrine receives its correct application and obtains its due result.

There is no sadder spectacle than this transformation of the Christian religion from a worship of God in spirit and in truth into a worship of God in signs, formulas, and idols. To feel the whole pity of this development, we need not descend to such adherents of this form of Christendom as are religiously and intellectually in a state of complete abandonment, like the Copts and Abyssinians; the Syrians, Greeks, and Russians are, taken as a whole, only a little better. Where, however, can we find in Jesus' message even a trace of any injunction that a man is to submit to solemn ceremonies as though they were mysterious ministrations, to be punctilious in observing a ritual, to put up pictures, and to mumble maxims and formulas in a prescribed fashion? *It was to destroy this sort of religion that Jesus Christ suffered himself to be nailed to the cross*, and now we find it re-established under his name and authority! Not only has "mystagogy" stepped into a position side by side with the "mathesis," that is to say, the doctrine, which called it forth; but the truth is that "doctrine"—be its constitution what it may, it is still a spiritual principle—has disappeared, and ceremony dominates everything. This is what marks the relapse into the ancient form of the lowest class of religion. Over the vast area of Greek and Oriental Christendom religion has been almost stifled by ritualism. It is not that religion has sacrificed one of its essential elements. No! it has entered an entirely different plane; it has descended to the level where religion may be described as a cult and nothing but a cult.

Nevertheless, Greek and Oriental Christianity contains within itself an element which for centuries has been capable of offering, and still offers here and there to-day, a certain resistance to the combined forces of traditionalism, intellectualism, and ritualism —I mean monasticism. To the question, Who is in the highest sense of the word a Christian? the Greek Christian replies : the monk. The man who practises silence and purity, who shuns not only the world but also the Church of the world, who avoids not only false doctrine but any statement about the true, who fasts, gives himself up to contemplation, and steadily waits for God's glorious light to dawn upon his gaze, who attaches no value to anything but tranquillity and meditation on the Eternal, who asks nothing of life but death, and in such complete un-selfishness and purity discovers the fountain of mercy—this is the Christian. To him not even the Church or the consecration which it bestows is an absolute necessity. For such a man the whole system of sanctified secularity has vanished. Over and over again in ascetics of this kind has the Church numbered in its ranks men of such strength and delicacy of religious feeling, so filled with the divine, so inwardly active in forming them-selves after certain features of Christ's image, that we may, indeed, say: here there is a living religion, not unworthy of Christ's name. We Protestants must not take direct offence at the form of monasticism. The conditions under which our Churches arose have made a harsh and one-sided opinion of it a kind of duty. And although for the present, and in view of the problems which press on us, we may be justified in retaining this opinion, we must not summarily apply it to other circum-stances. Nothing but monasticism could provide a leaven and a counterpoise in that traditionalistic and ritualistic secular Church, such as the Greek Church was and still is. Here there was freedom, independence, and vivid experience; here the truth that it is only what is experienced and comes from within that has any value in religion carried the day.

And yet, the invaluable tension which in this part of Christendom existed between the secular Church and monasticism has unhappily almost disappeared, and of the blessings which it imparted there is scarcely a trace left. Not only has monasticism become subject to the Church and is everywhere bent under its yoke, but the secular spirit has in a special degree invaded the monasteries. Greek and Oriental monks are now, as a rule, the instruments of the lowest and worst functions of the Church, of the worship of pictures and relics, of the crassest superstition and the most imbecile sorcery. Exceptions are not wanting, and it is still to the monks that we must pin our hopes of a better future; but it is not easy to see how a church is to be reformed which, teach what it will, is content with its adherents finding the Christian *faith* in the observance of certain ceremonies and Christian *morality* in keeping fast-days correctly.

As to our last question: What modifications did the Gospel undergo in this Church and how did it hold its own? Well, in the first place, I do not expect to be contradicted if I answer that this official ecclesiasticism with its priests and its cult, with all its vessels, saints, vestments, pictures and amulets, with its ordinances of fasting and its festivals, has absolutely nothing to do with the religion of Christ. It is the religion of the ancient world, tacked on to certain conceptions in the Gospel; or, rather, it is the ancient religion with the Gospel absorbed into it. The religious moods which are here produced, or which turn towards this kind of religion, are, in so far as they can still be called religious at all, of a class lower than Christian. But neither have its traditionalism and its "orthodoxy" much in common with the Gospel; they, too, were not derived from it and cannot be traced back to it. Correct doctrine, reverence, obedience, the shudderings of awe, may be valuable and edifying things; they may avail to bind and restrain the individual, especially when they draw him into the community of a stable society; but they have nothing to do with the Gospel, as long as they fail to touch the individual at the point where freedom lies, and inner decision for or against God. In contrast with this, monasticism, in its resolve to serve God by an ascetic and contemplative life, contains an incomparably more valuable element, because sayings of Christ, even though applied in a one-sided and limited way, are nevertheless taken as a standard, and the possibility of an independent inner life being kindled is not so far removed.

Not so far removed—entirely lacking, thank God, it is not, even in the waste shrines of this ecclesiasticism, and Christ's sayings sound in the ear of any who visit its churches. On the Church as a Church, apparatus and all, there is nothing more favourable to be said than has been said already; the best thing about it is that *it keeps up, although to a modest extent, the knowledge of the Gospel.* Jesus' words, even though only mumbled by the priests, take the first place in this Church, too, and the quiet mission which they carry out continues. Side by side with the magical apparatus and the transports of feeling, of which the ceremony is only the *caput mortuum*, stand Jesus' sayings; they are read in private and in public, and no superstition avails to destroy their power. Nor can its fruits be mistaken by anyone who will look below the surface. Among these Christians, too, priests and laity, there are men who have come to know God as the Father of mercy and the leader of their lives, and who love Jesus Christ, not because they know him as the person with two natures, but because a ray of his being has shone from the Gospel into their hearts, and this ray has become light and warmth to their own lives. And although the idea of the fatherly providence of God more readily assumes an almost fatalistic form in the East, and produces too much quietism, it is certain that here, too, it endows men with strength and energy, unselfishness and love. I need only refer again to Tolstoi's *Village Tales*, which I have already quoted. The picture which they present is not artificial. But from much also that I have myself seen and experienced I can testify how even with the Russian peasant or the humbler priests, in spite of all the Saint- and picture-worship, a power of simple trust in God is to be found, a delicacy of moral feeling, and an active brotherly love, which does not disclaim its origin in the Gospel. Where they exist, however, the entire ceremonial service of religion is capable of undergoing a spiritualisation, not by any "symbolical re-interpretation"—that is much too artificial a process—but because, if only the soul is touched by the living God at all, thought can rise to Him even by the help of an idol.

But it is truly no accidental circumstance that, in so far as any independent religious life is to be found among the members of this Church, it at once takes shape in trust in God, in humility, in unselfishness and mercy, and that Jesus Christ is at the same time laid hold of with reverence; for these are just the indications which show us that the Gospel is not as yet stifled, and that it is in these religious virtues that it has its real substance.

As a whole and in its structure the system of the Oriental Churches is foreign to the Gospel; it means at once a veritable transformation of the Christian faith and the depression of religion to a much lower level, namely, that of the ancient world. But in its monasticism, in so far as this is not entirely subject to the secular Church and itself secularised, there is an element which reduces the whole ecclesiastical apparatus to a secondary position, and which opens up the possibility of attaining a state of Christian independence. Above all, however, by not having suppressed the Gospel, but by having kept it accessible, even though in a meagre fashion, the Church still possesses the corrective in its midst. Side by side with the Church the Gospel exercises its own influence on individuals. This influence, however, takes shape in a type of religion exhibiting the very characteristics which we have shown to be most distinctive of Jesus' message. Thus on the ground occupied by this Church the Gospel has not completely perished. Here, too, human souls find a dependence on God and a freedom in Him, and when they have found these, they speak the language which every Christian understands, and which goes to every Christian's heart.

LECTURE FOURTEEN

THE CHRISTIAN RELIGION IN ROMAN CATHOLICISM

THE ROMAN Church is the most comprehensive and the vastest, the most complicated and yet at the same time the most uniform structure which, as far as we know, history has produced. All the powers of the human mind and soul, and all the elemental forces at mankind's disposal, have had a hand in creating it. In its many sided character and severe cohesion Roman Catholicism is far in advance of Greek. We ask in turn :

What did the Roman Catholic Church achieve?

What are its characteristics?

What modifications has the Gospel suffered in this Church, and how much of it has remained?

What did the Roman Catholic Church achieve? Well, in the first place, it educated the Romano-Germanic nations, and educated them in a sense other than that in which the Eastern Church educated the Greeks, Slavs, and Orientals. However much their original nature, or primitive and historical circumstances, may have favoured those nations and helped to promote their rise, the value of the services which the Church rendered is not thereby diminished. It brought Christian civilisation to young nations, and brought it, not once only, so as to keep them at its first stage—no! it gave them something which was capable of exercising a progressive educational influence, and for a period of almost a thousand years it itself led the advance. Up to the fourteenth century it was a leader and a mother; it supplied the ideas, set the aims, and disengaged the forces. Up to the fourteenth century—thenceforward, as we may see, those whom it educated became independent, and struck out paths which it did not indicate, and on which it is neither willing nor able to

follow them. But even so, however, during the period covered
by the last six hundred years, it has not fallen so far behind as
the Greek Church. Except for comparatively brief periods it has
proved itself fully a match for the whole movement of politics—
we in Germany know that well enough!—and even in the movement of thought it still has an important share. The time, of
course, is long past since it was a leader; on the contrary, it is
now a drag; but, in view of the mistaken and precipitate elements
in modern progress, the drag which it supplies is not always the
reverse of a blessing.

In the second place, however, this Church upheld the idea of
religious and ecclesiastical independence in Western Europe in
the face of the tendencies, not lacking here either, towards State
omnipotence in the spiritual domain. In the Greek Church, as
we saw, religion has become so intimately allied with nationality
and the State that, public worship and monasticism apart, it has
no room left for independent action. On Western ground it is
otherwise; the religious element and the moral element bound up
with it occupy an independent sphere and jealously guard it.
This we owe in the main to the Roman Church.

These two facts embrace the most important piece of work
which this Church achieved and in part still achieves. We have
already indicated the bounds which must be set to the first. To
the second also a sensible limitation attaches, and we shall see
what it is as we proceed.

What are the characteristics of the Roman Church? This
was our second question. Unless I am mistaken, the Church,
complicated as it is, may be resolved into three chief elements.
The first, *Catholicism*, it shares with the Greek Church. The
second is the *Latin spirit* and the *Roman World-empire* continuing in the Roman Church. The third is the spirit and religious
fervour of *St. Augustine*. So far as the inner life of this Church
is religious life and religious thought, it follows the standard
which St. Augustine authoritatively fixed. Not only has he arisen
again and again in his many successors, but he has awakened
and kindled numbers of men who, coming forward with

independent religious and theological fervour, are nevertheless
spirit of his spirit.

These three features, the Catholic, the Latin in the sense of
the Roman World-empire, and the Augustinian, constitute the
peculiar character of the Roman Church.

So far as the first is concerned, you may recognise its importance by the fact that the Roman Church to-day receives every
Greek Christian, nay, at once effects a "union" with every Greek
ecclesiastical community, without more ado, as soon as the Pope
is acknowledged and submission is made to his apostolic
supremacy. Any other condition that may be exacted from the
Greek Christians is of absolutely no moment; they are even
allowed to retain divine worship in their mother tongue, and
married priests. If we consider what a "purification" Protestants
have to undergo before they can be received into the bosom of
the Roman Church, the difference is obvious. Now a Church
cannot make so great a mistake about itself as to omit any essential condition in taking up new members, especially if they come
from another confession. The element which the Roman Church
shares with the Greek must, then, be of significant and critical
importance, when it is sufficient to make union possible on the
condition that the papal supremacy is recognised. As a matter
of fact, the main points characteristic of Greek Catholicism are
all to be found in Roman as well, and are, on occasion, just as
energetically maintained here as they are there. Traditionalism,
orthodoxy, and ritualism play just the same part here as they
do there, so far as "higher considerations" do not step in; and
the same is true of monasticism also.

So far as "higher considerations" do not step in—here we
have already passed to the examination of the second element,
namely, the Latin spirit in the sense of the Roman World-
dominion. In the Western half of Christendom the Latin spirit,
the spirit of Rome, very soon effected certain distinct modifications in the general Catholic idea. As early as the beginning
of the third century we see the thought emerging in the Latin
Fathers that salvation, however effected and whatever its nature,
is bestowed in the form of a contract under definite conditions,
and only to the extent to which they are observed; it is *salus*

legitima; in fixing these conditions the Deity manifested his mercy and indulgence, but it guards their observance all the more jealously. Further, the whole content of revelation is *lex,* the Bible as well as tradition. Again, this tradition is attached to a class of officials and to their correct succession. The "mysteries," however, are "sacraments"; that is to say, on the one hand they are binding acts; on the other, they contain definite gifts of grace in a carefully limited form and with a specific application. Again, the discipline of penance is a procedure laid down by law and akin to the process adopted in a civil action or a suit in defence of honour. Lastly, the Church is a *legal institution*; and it is so, not side by side with its function of preserving and distributing salvation, but it is a legal institution for the sake of this very function.

But it is in its constitution as a Church that it is a legal establishment. We must briefly see how things stand in regard to this constitution, as its foundations are common to the Eastern and the Western Church. When the monarchical episcopate had developed, the Church began to approximate its constitution to State government. The system of uniting sees under a metropolitan who was, as a rule, the bishop of the provincial capital, corresponded with the distribution of the empire into provinces. Above and beyond this, the ecclesiastical constitution in the East was developed a step further when it adapted itself to the division of the empire introduced by Diocletian, by which large groups of provinces were united. Thus arose the constitution of the patriarchate, which was not, however, strictly enforced, and was in part counteracted by other considerations.

In the West no division into patriarchates came about; but, on the other hand, something else happened : in the fifth century the Western Roman empire perished of internal weakness and through the inroads of the barbarians. What was left of what was Roman took refuge in the Roman Church—civilisation, law, and orthodox faith as opposed to the Arian. The barbarian chiefs, however, did not venture to set themselves up as Roman emperors and enter the vacant shrine of the *imperium*; they founded empires of their own in the provinces. In these circumstances the Bishop of Rome appeared as the guardian of the past and the shield of the future. All over the provinces occupied by the barbarians, even in those which had previously maintained a defiant independence in the face of Rome, bishops and laity looked to him. Whatever Roman elements the barbarians and Arians left standing in the provinces—and they were not few—were ecclesiasticised and at the same time put under the protection of the Bishop of Rome, who was the chief person there after the emperor's disappearance. But in Rome the episcopal throne was occupied in the fifth century by men who understood the signs of the times and utilised them to the full. *The Roman Church in this way privily pushed itself into the place of the Roman World-empire, of which it is the actual continuation;* the empire has not perished, but has only undergone a transformation. If we assert, and mean the assertion to hold good even of the present time, that the Roman Church is the old *Roman empire* consecrated by the Gospel, that is no mere "clever remark," but the recognition of the true state of the matter historically, and the most appropriate and fruitful way of describing the character of this Church. It still governs the nations; its Popes rule like Trajan and Marcus Aurelius; Peter and Paul have taken the place of Romulus and Remus; the bishops and arch-bishops, of the proconsuls; the troops of priests and monks correspond to the legions; the Jesuits, to the imperial bodyguard. The continued influence of the old empire and its institutions may be traced in detail, down to individual legal ordinances, nay, even in the very clothes. That is no Church like the Protestant communities, or the national Churches of the East; it is a political creation, and as imposing as a World-empire, because the continuation of the Roman empire. The Pope, who calls himself "King" and "Pontifex Maximus," is Cæsar's successor. The Church, which as early as the third and fourth century was entirely filled with the Roman spirit, has re-established in itself the Roman empire. Nor have patriotic Catholics in Rome and Italy in every century from the seventh and eighth onwards understood the matter otherwise. When Gregory VII entered upon the struggle with the imperial power, this is the way in which an Italian prelate fired his ardour :

Seize the first Apostle's sword,
  Peter's glowing sword, and smite!
Scatter far the savage horde;
  Break their wild, impetuous might!
Let them feel the yoke of yore.
Let them bear it evermore!

What with blood in Marius' day,
  Marius and his soldiers brave,
Or by Julius' mighty sway,
  Romans did their land to save;
Thou canst do by simple word.
Great the Church's holy sword!

Rome made great again by thee
  Offers all thy meed of praise;
Not for Scipio's victory
  Did it louder pæans raise,
Nor entwine the laurel crown
For a deed of more renown.

Who is it that is thus addressed, a bishop or a Cæsar? A Cæsar, I imagine, or, rather, a priestly Cæsar; it was felt to be so then, and it is still felt to be so to-day. It is an *Empire* that this priestly Cæsar rules, and to attack it with the armament of dogmatic polemics alone is to beat the air.

I cannot here show what immense results follow from the fact that the Catholic Church is the Roman empire. Let me mention only a few conclusions which the Church itself draws. *It is just as essential to this Church to exercise governmental power as to proclaim the Gospel.* The phrase "Christus vincit, Christus regnat, Christus triumphat," must be understood in a political sense. He rules on earth by the fact that his Rome-directed Church rules, and rules, too, by law and by force; that is to say, it employs all the means of which States avail themselves. Accordingly it recognises no form of religious fervour which does not first of all submit to this papal Church, is approved by it, and remains in constant dependence upon it. This Church, then, teaches its "subjects" to say: "Though I understand all mysteries, and though I have all faith, and though I bestow all my goods to feed the poor, and though I give my body to be burned, and have not unity in love which alone floweth from unconditional obedience to the Church, it profiteth me nothing." Outside the pale of the Church, all faith, all love, all the virtues, even martyrdoms, are of no value whatever. Naturally; for even an earthly State appreciates only those services which a man has rendered for its sake. But here the State identifies itself with the kingdom of heaven, in other respects proceeding just like other States. From this fact you can yourselves deduce all the Church's claims; they follow without difficulty. Even the most exorbitant demand appears quite natural as soon as you only admit the truth of the two leading propositions: "The Roman Church is the kingdom of God," and "The Church must govern like an earthly State." It is not to be denied that Christian motives have also had a hand in this development—the desire to bring the Christian religion into a real connexion with life, and to make its influence felt in every situation that may arise, as well as anxiety for the salvation of individuals and of nations. How many earnest Catholic Christians there have been who had no other real desire than to establish Christ's rule on earth and build up his kingdom! But while there can be no doubt that their intention, and the energy with which they put their hands to the work, made them superior to the Greeks, there can be as little that it is a serious misunderstanding of Christ's and the apostle's injunctions to aim at establishing and building up the kingdom of God by political means. The only forces which this kingdom knows are religious and moral forces, and it rests on a basis of freedom. But when a Church comes forward with the claims of an earthly State, it is bound to make use of all the means at the disposal of that State, including, therefore, crafty diplomacy and force; for the earthly State, even a State governed by law, must on occasion become a State that acts contrary to law. The course of development which this Church has followed as an earthly State was, then, bound to lead logically to the absolute monarchy of the Pope and his infallibility; for in an earthly theocracy infallibility means, at bottom, nothing more than full sovereignty means in a secular State. That the Church has not shrunk from drawing this last conclusion is a proof of the extent to which the sacred element in it has become secularised.

That this second element was bound to produce a radical change in the characteristic features of Catholicism in Western Europe, in its traditionalism, its orthodoxy, its ritualism, and its monasticism, is obvious. Traditionalism holds the same position after the change as it did before; but when any element in it has become inconvenient, it is dropped and its place taken by the papal will. "La tradition, c'est moi," as Pius IX is reported to have said. Further, "sound doctrine" is still a leading principle, but, as a matter of fact, it can be altered by the ecclesiastical policy of the Pope; subtle distinctions have given many a dogma a new meaning. New dogmas, too, are promulgated. In many respects doctrine has become more arbitrary, and a rigid formula in a matter of dogma may be set aside by a contrary injunction in a matter of ethics and in the confessional. The hard and fast lines of the past can be everywhere relaxed in favour of the needs of the present. The same holds good of ritualism, as also of monasticism. The extent to which the old monasticism has been altered, by no means always to its disadvantage alone, and has even in some important aspects been transformed into its flat opposite, I cannot here show. In its organisation this Church possesses a faculty of adapting itself to the course of history such as no other Church possesses; it always remains the same old Church, or seems to do so, and is always becoming a new one.

The third element determining the character of the spirit prevalent in the Church is opposed to that which we have just discussed, and yet has held its own side by side with the second : it goes by the names of *Augustine* and *Augustinianism*. In the fifth century, at the very time when the Church was setting itself to acquire the inheritance of the Roman empire, it came into possession of a religious genius of extraordinary depth and power, accepted his ideas and feelings, and up to the present day has been unable to get rid of them. That the Church became at one and the same time Cæsarian and Augustinian is the most important and marvellous fact in its history. What kind of a spirit, however, and what kind of a tendency, did it receive from Augustine?

Well, in the first place, *Augustine's theology and his religious fervour denote a special resuscitation of the Pauline experience and doctrine of sin and grace, of guilt and justification, of divine predestination and human servitude.* In the centuries that had elapsed since the apostle's day this experience and the doctrine embodying it had been lost, but Augustine went through the same inner experiences as Paul, gave them the same sort of expression, and clothed them in definite conceptions. There was no question here of mere imitation; the individual differences between the two cases are of the utmost importance, especially in the way in which the doctrine of justification is conceived. With Augustine, it was represented as a constant process, continuing until love and all the virtues completely filled the heart; but, as with Paul, it is all a matter of individual experience and inner life. If you read Augustine's *Confessions* you will acknowledge that in spite of all the rhetoric—and rhetoric there is—it is the work of a genius who has felt God, the God of the Spirit, to be the be-all and the end-all of his life : who thirsts after Him and desires nothing beside Him. Further, all the sad and terrible experiences which he had had in his own person, all the rupture with himself, all the service of transient things, the "crumbling away into the world bit by bit," and the egoism for which he had to pay in loss of strength and freedom, he reduces to the one root, *sin*; that is to say, lack of communion with God, godlessness. Again, what released him from the entanglements of the world, from selfishness and inner decay, and gave him strength, freedom, and a consciousness of the Eternal, he calls, with Paul, *grace*. With him he feels, too, that grace is wholly the work of God, but that it is obtained through and by Christ, and possessed as forgiveness of sins and as the spirit of love. He is much less free and more beset with scruples in his view of sin than the great apostle; and it is this which gives his religious language and everything that proceeded from him quite a peculiar colour. "Forgetting those things which are behind, and reaching forth unto those things which are before"—the apostolic maxim is not Augustine's. *Consolation for the misery of sin—* this is the complexion of his entire Christianity. Only rarely was he capable of soaring to the sense of the glorious liberty of the children of God; and, where he was so capable, he could not testify to it in the same way as Paul. But he could express the sense of consolation for the misery of sin with a strength of feeling and in words of an overwhelming force such as no one before him ever displayed; nay, more : he managed by what he wrote to go so straight to the souls of millions, to describe so precisely their inner condition, and so impressively and overpoweringly to put the consolation before them, that what he felt has been felt again and again for fifteen hundred years. *Up to the very day in which we live, so far as Catholic Christians are concerned, inward and vivid religious fervour, and the expression which it takes, are in their whole character Augustinian.* It is by what he felt that they are kindled, and it is his thoughts that they think. Nor is it otherwise with many Protestants, and those not of the worst kind. This juxtaposition of sin and grace, this interconnexion of feeling and doctrine, seems to possess an indestructible power which no lapse of time is able to touch; this feeling of mild pain and bliss is an unforgettable possession with those who have once experienced it; and even though they may have subsequently emancipated themselves from religion, it remains for them a sacred memory.

The Western Church opened, and was compelled to open, its doors to this Augustine at the very moment when it was preparing to enter upon its dominion. It was defenceless in face of him; it had so little of any real value to offer from its immediate past that it weakly capitulated. Thus arose the astonishing "complexio oppositorum" which we see in Western Catholicism : the Church of rites, of law, of politics, of World-dominion, and the Church in which a highly individual, delicate, sublimated sense and doctrine of sin and grace is brought into play. The external and the internal elements are supposed to unite! To speak frankly, this was impossible from the beginning; internal tension and conflict were bound to arise at once; the history of Western Catholicism is full of it. Up to a certain point, however, these antitheses admit of being reconciled; they admit of it at least so far as the same men are concerned. That is proved by no less a person than Augustine himself, who, in addition to his other characteristics, was also a staunch Churchman; nay, who in such matters as power and prestige promoted the external interests of the Church, and its equipment as a whole, with the greatest energy. I cannot here explain how he managed to accomplish this work, but that there could be no lack of internal contradictions in it is obvious. Only let us be clear about two facts; firstly, that the outward Church is more and more forcing the inward Augustinianism into the background, and transforming and modifying it, without, however, being able wholly to destroy it; secondly, that all the great personalities who have continued to kindle religious fervour afresh in the Western Church, and to purify and deepen it, have directly or indirectly proceeded from Augustine and formed themselves on him. The long chain of Catholic reformers, from Agobard and Claudius of Turin in the ninth century down to the Jansenists in the seventeenth and eighteenth, and beyond them, is Augustinian. And if the Council of Trent may in many respects be rightly called *a Council of Reform*; if the doctrine of penance and grace was formulated then with much more depth and inwardness than could be expected from the state of Catholic theology in the fourteenth and fifteenth centuries, that is only owing to the continued influence of Augustine. With the doctrine of grace taken from Augustine, the Church has, indeed, associated a practice of the confessional which threatens to make that doctrine absolutely ineffective. But however far it may stretch its bounds so as to keep all those within its pale who do not revolt against its authority, it after all not only tolerates such as take the same view of sin and grace as Augustine, but it also desires that, wherever possible, everyone may feel as strongly as he the gravity of sin and the blessedness of belonging to God.

Such are the essential elements of Roman Catholicism. There is much else that might be mentioned, but what has been said denotes the leading points.

We pass to the last question : What modifications has the Gospel here undergone, and how much of it is left? Well—this is not a matter that needs many words—the whole outward and visible institution of a Church *claiming divine dignity* has no foundation whatever in the Gospel. It is a case, not of distortion, but of total perversion. Religion has here strayed away in a direction that is not its own. As Eastern Catholicism may in many respects be more appropriately regarded as part of the history of Greek religion than of the history of the Gospel, so Roman Catholicism must be regarded as part of *the history of the Roman World-empire*. To contend, as it does, that Christ founded a kingdom; that this kingdom is the Roman Church; that he equipped it with a sword, nay, with two swords, a spiritual and a temporal, is to secularise the Gospel; nor can this contention be sustained by appealing to the idea that Christ's spirit ought certainly *to bear rule* amongst mankind. The Gospel says, "Christ's kingdom is not of this world," but the Church has set up an earthly kingdom; Christ demands that his ministers shall not rule but serve, but here the priests govern the world; Christ leads his disciples away from political and ceremonious religion and places every man face to face with God—God and the soul, the soul and its God—but here, on the contrary, man is bound to an earthly institution with chains that cannot be broken, and he must obey; it is only when he obeys that he approaches God. There was a time when Roman Christians shed their blood because they refused to do worship to Cæsar, and rejected religion of the political kind; to-day they do not, indeed, actually pray to an earthly ruler, but they have subjected their souls to the despotic orders of the Roman papal king.

LECTURE FIFTEEN

THE POINT to which we referred at the close of the last lecture was that, as an outward and visible Church and a State founded on law and on force, Roman Catholicism has nothing to do with the Gospel, nay, is in fundamental contradiction with it. That this State has borrowed a divine lustre from the Gospel, and finds this lustre extraordinarily advantageous, cannot avail to upset the verdict. To mingle the divine with the secular, and what is innermost in a man with a political element, is to work the greatest of mischiefs, because the conscience is thereby enslaved and religion robbed of its solemn character. It is inevitable that this character should be lost when every possible measure which serves to maintain the *earthly* empire of the Church—for example, the sovereignty of the Pope—is proclaimed as the divine will. We are reminded, however, that it is just this independent action on the part of the Church which saves religion in Western Europe from entirely degenerating into nationality or the State or police. The Church, it is urged, has maintained intact the high idea of the complete self-subsistence of religion and its independence of the State. We may admit the claim, but the price which Western Europe has had to pay for this service, and still pays, is much too great; by having to pay so heavy a tribute, the nations are threatened with bankruptcy *within*; and as for the Church, the capital which it has amassed is truly a capital that consumes. With all the apparent increase in its power, a pauperising process is being accomplished in the Church, slowly but surely. Let me here digress from our subject for a moment.

No one who looks at the present political situation can have any ground for asserting that the power of the Roman Church is on the wane. What a growth it has experienced in the nineteenth century! And yet—anyone with a keen eye sees that the

Church is far from possessing now such a plenitude of power as it enjoyed in the twelfth and thirteenth centuries, when all the material and spiritual forces available were at its disposal. Since that epoch its power has, *in point of intensity, suffered an enormous decline*, arrested by a few brief outbursts of enthusiasm between 1540 and 1620, and in the nineteenth century. Earnest Catholics, concerned at this fact, make no secret of it; they know and admit that an important portion of the spiritual possessions necessary to the dominion of the Church has been lost to it. And again; what is the position of the Latin nations which, when all is said, form the proper province of the Roman Church's rule? There is only one of them which can really be called a great Power, and what sort of spectacle will it present in another generation? As a State this Church lives to-day, to a not inconsiderable extent, on its history, its old Roman mediæval history; and it lives as the Roman empire of the Romans. But empires do not live for ever. Will the Church be capable of maintaining itself in the great changes to come? Will it bear the increasing tension between it and the intellectual life of the people? Will it survive the decline of the Latin nations?

But let us leave this question to answer itself. Let us recollect, rather, that this Church, thanks above all to its Augustinianism, possesses in its orders of monkhood and its religious societies a deep element of life in its midst. In all ages it has produced saints, so far as men can be so called, and it still produces them to-day. Trust in God, unaffected humility, the assurance of redemption, the devotion of one's life to the service of one's brethren, are to be found in it; many brethren take up the cross of Christ and exercise at one and the same time that self-judgment and that joy in God which Paul and Augustine achieved. The *Imitatio Christi* kindles independent religious life and a fire which burns with a flame of its own. Ecclesiasticism has not availed to suppress the power of the Gospel, which, in spite of the frightful weight that it has to carry, makes its way again and again. It still works like leaven, nor can we fail to see that this Church, side by side with a lax morality for which it has often enough been to blame, has, by the mouth of its great mediæval theologians, fruitfully applied the Gospel to many circumstances of life and created a Christian ethics. Here and elsewhere it has proved that it not only carries, as it were, the thoughts of the Gospel with it, as a river carries grains of gold, but that they are bound up with it and have been further developed in it. The infallible Pope, the "Apostolico-Roman polytheism," the veneration of the Saints, blind obedience and a pathetic devotion—these things seem to have stifled all inwardness, and yet there are Christians still to be found in this Church, too, of the kind which the Gospel has awakened, earnest and loving, filled with joy and peace in God. Lastly, the mischief is not that the Gospel has been bound up with political forms at all—Melanchthon was no traitor when he expressed his willingness to acknowledge the Pope if he would permit the Gospel to be preached in its purity—but it lies in the *sanctification* of the political element, and in the inability of this Church to get rid of what was once of service in particular historical circumstances, but has now become an obstruction and a clog.

We now pass to the last section in the exposition of our subject.

THE CHRISTIAN RELIGION IN PROTESTANTISM

Anyone who looks at the external condition of Protestantism, especially in Germany, may, at first sight, well exclaim : "What a miserable spectacle!" But no one can survey the history of Europe from the second century to the present time without being forced to the conclusion that in the whole course of this history the greatest movement and the one most pregnant with good was the Reformation in the sixteenth century; even the great change which took place at the transition to the nineteenth is inferior to it in importance. What do all our discoveries and inventions and our advances in outward civilisation signify in comparison with the fact that to-day there are thirty millions of Germans, and many more millions of Christians outside Germany, who possess a religion without priests, without sacrifices, without "fragments" of grace, without ceremonies—a spiritual religion !

Protestantism must be understood, first and foremost, by the contrast which it offers to Catholicism, and here there is a double direction which any estimate of it must take, first as *Reformation*

and secondly as *Revolution*. It was a reformation in regard to
the doctrine of salvation; a revolution in regard to the Church,
its authority, and its apparatus. Hence Protestantism is no spon-
taneous phenomenon, created as it were by a "generatio
equivoca"; but, as its very name implies, it was called into being
by the misdeeds of the Roman Church having become intolerable. It was the close of a long series of cognate but ineffectual
attempts at reform in the Middle Ages. If the position which it
thus holds in history proves its continuity with the past, the fact
is still more strongly in evidence in its own and not inappropriate
contention that it was not an innovation in regard to religion,
but a restoration and renewal of it. But from the point of view
of the Church and its authority, Protestantism was undoubtedly
a revolutionary phenomenon. We must, then, take account of
it in both these relations.

Protestantism was a *Reformation*, that is to say, a renewal
as regards the core of the matter, as regards religion, and consequently as regards the doctrine of salvation. That may be
shown in the main in three points.

In the first place, religion was here brought back again to
itself, in so far as the Gospel and the corresponding religious
experience were put into the foreground and freed of all alien
accretions. Religion was taken out of the vast and monstrous
fabric which had been previously called by its name—a fabric
embracing the Gospel and holy water, the priesthood of all
believers and the Pope on his throne, Christ the Redeemer and
St. Anne—and was *reduced* to its essential factors, to the Word
of God and to faith. This truth was imposed as a *criterion* on
everything that also claimed to be "religion" and to unite on
terms of equality with those great factors. In the history of
religion every really important reformation is always, first and
foremost, *a critical reduction* to principles; for in the course of
its historical development, religion, by adapting itself to circumstances, attracts to itself much alien matter, and produces, in
conjunction with this, a number of hybrid and apocryphal
elements, which it is necessarily compelled to place under the
protection of what is sacred. If it is not to run wild from exuberance, or be choked by its own dry leaves, the reformer must

come who purifies it and brings it back to itself. This critical reduction to principles Luther accomplished in the sixteenth century, by victoriously declaring that the Christian religion was given only in the Word of God and in the inward experience which accords with this Word.

In the *second* place, there was the definite way in which the "Word of God" and the "experience" of it were grasped. For Luther the "Word" did not mean Church doctrine; it did not even mean the Bible; it meant the message of the free grace of God in Christ which makes guilty and despairing men happy and blessed; and the "experience" was just the certainty of this grace. In the sense in which Luther took them, both can be embraced in one phrase : *the confident belief in a God of grace.* They put an end—such was his own experience, and such was what he taught—to all inner discord in a man; they overcome the burden of every ill; they destroy the sense of guilt; and, despite the imperfection of a man's own acts, they give him the certainty of being inseparably united with the Holy God :

> Now I know and believe
>   And give praise without end
> That God the Almighty
>   Is Father and Friend,
> And that in all troubles,
>   Whatever betide,
> He hushes the tempest
>   And stands at my side.

Nothing, he taught, is to be preached but the God of Grace, with whom we are reconciled through Christ. Conversely, it is not a question of ecstasies and visions; no transports of feeling are necessary; it is *faith* that is to be aroused. Faith is to be the beginning, middle, and end of all religious fervour. In the correspondence of Word and faith "justification" is experienced and hence justification holds the chief place in the Reformer's message; it means nothing less than the attainment of peace and freedom in God through Christ, dominion over the world, and an eternity within.

Lastly, the third feature of this renewal was the great transformation which *God's worship* now inevitably underwent, God's worship by the individual and by the community. Such worship—this was obvious—can and ought to be nothing but putting *faith* to practical proof. As Luther declared over and over again, "all that God asks of us is faith, and it is through faith alone that he is willing to treat with us." To let God be God, and to pay Him honour by acknowledging and invoking Him as Father—it is thus alone that a man can serve Him. Every other path on which a man tries to approach Him and honour Him leads astray, and vain is the attempt to establish any other relation with Him. What an enormous mass of anxious, hopeful, and hopeless effort was now done away with, and what a revolution in worship was effected! But all that is true of God's worship by the individual is true in exactly the same way of public worship. Here, too, it is only the Word of God and prayer which have any place. All else is to be banished; the community assembled for God's worship is to proclaim the message of God with praise and thanksgiving, and call upon His name. Anything that goes beyond this is not worship at all.

These three points embrace the chief elements in the Reformation. What they involved was a *renewal* of religion; for not only do they denote, albeit in a fashion of their own, a return to Christianity as it originally was, but they also existed themselves in Western Catholicism, although buried in a heap of rubbish.

But, before we go further, permit me two brief digressions. We were just saying that the community assembled for God's worship must not solemnise its worship in any other way than by proclaiming the Word and by prayer. To this, however, we must add, according to the Reformers' injunctions, that all that is to stamp this community as a Church is its existence as a community of the faith in which God's Word is preached aright. Here we may leave the sacraments out of account, as, according to Luther, they, too, derive their entire importance from the Word. But if Word and faith are the only characteristics of worship, it looks as if those who contend that the Reformation did away with the visible Church and put an invisible one in its place were right. But the contention does not tally with the facts. The distinction between a visible and an invisible Church dates back as far as the Middle Ages, or even, from one point of view, as far as Augustine. Those who defined the true Church as "the number of the predestined" were obliged to maintain that it was wholly invisible. But the German Reformers did not so define it. In declaring the Church to be a community of the faith in which God's Word is preached aright, they rejected all the coarser characteristics of a Church, and certainly excluded the visibility that appeals to the senses; but—to take an illustration—who would say that an intellectual community, for example, a band of young men all alike eagerly devoted to knowledge or the interests of their country, was "invisible," because it possesses no external characteristics, and cannot be counted on one's fingers? Just as little is the evangelical Church an "invisible" community. It is a community of the spirit, and therefore its "visibility" takes different phases and different degrees of strength. There are phases of it where it is absolutely unrecognisable, and others, again, where it stands forth with the energy of a power that appeals to the senses. It can never, indeed, take the sharp contours of a State like the Venetian republic or the kingdom of France—such was the comparison which a great exponent of Catholic dogmatics declared to be applicable to his Church—but as Protestants we ought to know that we belong, not to an "invisible" Church, but to a spiritual community which disposes of the forces pertaining to spiritual communities—a spiritual community resting on earth, but reaching to the Eternal.

And now as to the other point: Protestantism maintains that, objectively, the Christian community is based upon the Gospel alone, but that the Gospel is contained in Holy Scripture. From the very beginning it has encountered the objection that, if that be so, and at the same time there be no recognised authority to decide what the purport and meaning of the Gospel is and how it is to be ascertained from the Scriptures, general confusion will be the result; that of this confusion the history of Protestantism affords ample testimony; that if every man has a warrant to decide what the "true understanding" of the Gospel is, and in this respect is bound to no tradition, no council, and no pope, but exercises the free right of research, any unity, community, or Church is absolutely impossible; that the State, therefore, must interfere, or some arbitrary limit be fixed. That no Church possessing the Sacred Office of the Inquisition can arise in this way is certainly true; further, that to impose any *external* limits on a community *from the inside* is a simple impossibility. What has been done by the State or under pressure of historical necessities does not affect the question at all; the structures which have arisen in this way are, in the Protestant sense, only figuratively called "Churches." *Protestantism reckons*—this is the solution—*upon the Gospel being something so simple, so divine, and therefore so truly human, as to be most certain of being understood when it is left entirely free, and also as to produce essentially the same experiences and convictions in individual souls.* In this it may often enough make mistakes; differences of individuality and education may issue in very heterogeneous results; but still, in this its attitude, it has not up to now been put to shame. A real, spiritual community of Protestant Christians; a common conviction as to what is most important and as to its application to life in all its forms, has arisen and is in full force and vigour. This community embraces Protestants in and outside Germany, Lutherans, Calvinists, and adherents of other denominations. In all of them, so far as they are earnest Christians, there lives a common element, and this element is of infinitely greater importance and value than all their differences. It keeps us to the Gospel and it protects us from modern heathenism and from relapse into Catholicism. More than this we do not need; nay, any other fetter we reject. This, however, is no fetter, but the condition of our freedom. And when we are reproached with our divisions and told that Protestantism has as many doctrines as heads, we reply, "So it has, but we do not wish it otherwise; on the contrary, we want still more freedom, still greater individuality in utterance and in doctrine; the historical circumstances necessitating the formation of national and free churches have imposed only too many rules and limitations upon us, even though they be not proclaimed as divine ordinances; we want still more confidence in the inner strength and unifying power of the Gospel, which is more certain to prevail in free conflict than under guardianship; we want to be a spiritual realm and we have no desire to return to the fleshpots of Egypt; we are well aware that in the interests of order and instruction outward and visible communities must arise; we are ready to foster their growth, so far as they fulfil these aims and deserve to be fostered; but we do not hang our hearts upon them, for they may exist to-day and to-morrow give place, under other political or social conditions, to new organisations; let anyone who has such a Church have it as though he had it not; our Church is not the particular Church in which we are placed, but the 'societas fidei' which has its members everywhere, even among Greeks and Romans." That is the Protestant answer to the reproach that we are "divided," and that is the language which the liberty which has been given to us employs. Let us now return from these digressions to the exposition of the essential features of Protestantism.

Protestantism was not only a Reformation but also a *Revolution*. From the legal point of view the whole Church system against which Luther revolted could lay claim to full obedience. It had just as much legal validity in Western Europe as the laws of the State themselves. When Luther burned the papal bull he undoubtedly performed a revolutionary act—revolutionary, not in the bad sense of a revolt against legal ordinance which is also moral ordinance as well, but certainly in the sense of a violent breach with a given legal condition. It was against this state of things that the new movement was directed, and it was to the following chief points that its protest in word and deed extended. Firstly: It protested against the entire hierarchical and priestly system in the Church, demanded that it should be abolished, and abolished it in favour of a common priesthood and an established order formed on the basis of the congregation. What a range this demand had, and to what an extent it interfered with the previously existing state of things, cannot be told in a few sentences. To explain it all would take hours. Nor can we here show how the various arrangements actually took shape in the Protestant churches. That is not a matter of fundamental importance, but what is of fundamental importance is that *the "divine" rights of the Church were abolished*.

Secondly: It protested against all formal, external authority in religion; against the authority, therefore, of councils, priests, and the whole tradition of the Church. That alone is to be authority which shows itself to be such within and effects a deliverance: the thing itself, therefore, the Gospel. Thus Luther also protested against the authority of the letter of the Bible; but we shall see that this was a point on which neither he nor the rest of the Reformers were quite clear, and where they failed to draw the conclusions which their insight into fundamentals demanded.

Thirdly: It protested against all the traditional arrangements for public worship, all ritualism, and every sort of "holy work." As it neither knows nor tolerates, as we have seen, any specific form of worship, any material sacrifice and service to God, any mass and any works done for God and with a view to salvation, the whole traditional system of public worship, with its pomp, its holy and semi-holy articles, its gestures and processions, came to the ground. How much could be retained in the way of form for *æsthetic* or *educational* reasons was, in comparison with this, a question of entirely secondary importance.

Fourthly: It protested against Sacramentalism. Baptism and the Lord's Supper it left standing, as institutions of the primitive Church, or, as it might be, of the Lord himself; but it desired that they should be regarded either as symbols and marks by which the Christian is known, or as acts deriving their value exclusively from that message of the forgiveness of sins which is bound up with them. All other sacraments it abolished, and with them the whole notion of God's grace and help being accessible in bits, and fused in some mysterious way with definite corporeal things. To sacramentalism it opposed the *Word*, and to the notion that grace was given by bits the conviction that there is only one grace, namely, to possess *God Himself* as the source of grace. It was not because Luther was so very enlightened that in his tract *"On the Babylonian Captivity"* he rejected the whole system of Sacramentalism—he had enough superstition left in him to enable him to advance some very shocking contentions—but because he had had inner experience of the fact that where "grace" does not endow the soul with the living God Himself it is an illusion. Hence for him the whole doctrine of sacramentalism was an infringement of God's majesty and an enslavement of the soul.

Fifthly: It protested against the double form of morality, and accordingly against the "higher" form; against the contention that it is particularly well-pleasing to God to make no use of the powers and gifts which are part of creation. The Reformers had a strong sense of the fact that the world passes away with the lusts thereof; we must certainly not represent Luther as the modern man cheerfully standing with his feet firmly planted on the earth; on the contrary, like the men of the Middle Ages he had a strong yearning to be rid of this world and to depart from the "vale of tears." But because he was convinced that we neither can nor ought to offer God anything but Trust in Him, he arrived, in regard to the Christian's position in the world, at quite different opinions from those which were advanced by the grave monks of previous centuries. As fastings and ascetic practices had no value before God, and were of no advantage to one's fellowmen, and as God is the Creator of all things, the most useful thing that a man can do is to remain in the position in which God has placed him. This conviction gave Luther a cheerful and confident view of earthly ordinances, which contrasts with and actually got the upper hand of his inclination to turn his back upon the world. He advanced the definite opinion that all positions in life—constituted authority, the married state, and so on, down to domestic service—existed by the will of God, and were therefore genuinely spiritual positions in which we are to serve God; a faithful maidservant stands higher, with him, than a contemplative monk. Christians are not to be always devising how they may find some new paths of their own, but to show patience and love of neighbour within the sphere of their given vocation. Out of this there grew up in his mind the notion that all worldly laws and spheres of activity have an independent title. It is not that they are to be merely tolerated, and have no right to exist until they receive it from the Church. No! they have rights of their own, and they form the vast domain in which the Christian is to give proof of his faith and love; nay, they are even to be respected in places which are as yet ignorant of God's revelation in the Gospel.

It was thus that the same man who asked nothing of the world, so far as his own personal feelings were concerned, and whose soul was troubled only by thought for the Eternal, delivered mankind from the ban of asceticism. He was thereby really and truly the life and origin of a new epoch, and he gave it back a simple and unconstrained attitude towards the world, and a good conscience in all earthly labour. This fruitful work fell to his share, not because he secularised religion, but because he took it so seriously and so profoundly that, while in his view it was to pervade all things, it was itself to be freed from everything external to it.

LECTURE SIXTEEN

THE QUESTION has often been raised whether, and to what extent, the Reformation was a work of the *German* spirit. I cannot here go into this complicated problem. But this much seems to me to be certain, that while we cannot, indeed, connect Luther's momentous religious experiences with his nationality, the results, positive as well as negative, with which he invested them display the German—the *German* man and *German* history. From the time that the Germans endeavoured to make themselves really at home in the religion handed down to them —this did not take place until the thirteenth century onwards— they were preparing the way for the Reformation. And just as Eastern Christianity is rightly called *Greek*, and the Christianity of the Middle Ages and of Western Europe is rightly called *Roman*, so the Christianity of the Reformation may be described as *Germanic*, in spite of Calvin. For Calvin was Luther's pupil, and he made his influence most lastingly felt, not among the Latin nations but among the English, the Scotch, and the Dutch. Through the Reformation the Germans mark a stage in the history of the Universal Church. No similar statement can be made of the Slavs.

The recoil from asceticism, which as an ideal never penetrated the Germans to the same extent as other nations, and the protest against religion as external authority, are to be set down as well to the Pauline Gospel as to the German spirit. Luther's warmth and heartiness in preaching, and his frankness in polemical utterance, were felt by the German nation to be an opening out of its own soul.

In the previous lecture we touched upon the chief provinces in which Luther raised an emphatic and still effective protest. There is much upon which I could also dwell: for example,

upon the opposition which, especially at the commencement of
his reforming activity, he offered to the whole terminology of
dogmatics, its formula and doctrinal utterances. To sum up :
he protested, because his aim was to restore the Christian religion
in its purity, without priests and sacrifices, without external
authorities and ordinances, without solemn ceremonies, without
all the chains with which the Beyond was to be bound to the
Here. In its revising ardour the Reformation went back not only
earlier than the eleventh century, not only earlier than the fourth
or the second, but to the very beginnings of religion. Nay, without
being aware of it, the Reformation even modified or entirely
put aside forms which existed even in the apostolic age : thus
in matters of discipline it abolished fasting; in matters of constitution it abolished bishops and deacons; in matters of doctrine
it abolished, among other things, Chiliasm.

But with the change effected by Reformation and Revolution,
how does the new creation stand *as a whole* in regard to the
Gospel? We may say that in the four leading points which we
emphasised in the previous lecture—inwardness and spirituality,
the fundamental thought of the God of grace, His worship in
spirit and in truth, and the idea of the Church as a community
of faith—the Gospel was in reality re-won. Need I prove this
in detail, or are we to be shaken in our conviction because, as is
surely the case, a Christian in the sixteenth and in the nineteenth
century presents an appearance different from that which a
Christian presented in the first? That the inwardness and individualism which the Reformation disengaged accord with the
character of the Gospel is certain. Further, Luther's pronouncement on justification not only reflects in the main, and in spite
of certain irreducible differences, Paul's train of thought, but is
also in point of aim in exact correspondence with Jesus' teaching.
To know God as one's Father, to possess a God of grace, to find
comfort in His grace and providence, to believe in the forgiveness
of sins—in both cases that is the point on which everything turns.
And in the troubled times of Lutheran orthodoxy a Paul
Gerhardt succeeded in giving such grand expression to this
fundamental conviction of the Gospel in his hymns, "Is God

for me? Then let all," and "Commit thy ways," as to convince
us how truly Protestantism was penetrated with it. Again, that
the right worship of God ought to be nothing but the acknow-
ledgment of God in praise and prayer, and that the love of
neighbour is also worship, is taken direct from the Gospel and
Paul's corresponding injunctions. Lastly, that the true Church
is held together by the Holy Ghost and by faith; that it is a
spiritual community of brothers and sisters, is a conviction which
is in line with the Gospel, and was most clearly expressed by
Paul. In so far as the Reformation restored all this, and also
recognised Christ as the only Redeemer, it may in the strictest
sense of the word be called *evangelical*; and in so far as these
convictions, crippled and burdened though they may be, retain
their ascendancy in the Protestant Churches, they have every
warrant for being so described.

But what was here achieved had its dark side as well. If we
ask what the Reformation cost us, and to what extent it made
its principles prevail, we shall see this dark side very clearly.

We get nothing from history without paying for it, and for a
violent movement we have to pay double. What did the Reformation cost us? I will not speak of the fact that the unity of
Western civilisation was destroyed, since it was after all only
over a part of Western Europe that the Reformation prevailed,
for the freedom and many-sided character of the resulting
development brought us a greater gain. But the necessity of
establishing the new Churches as *State-Churches* was attended
by serious disadvantages. The system of an ecclesiastical State
is, of course, worse, and its adherents have truly no cause to
praise it in contrast with the State-Churches. But still the latter—
which are not solely the outcome of the breach with ecclesiastical
authority, but were already prepared for in the fifteenth century
—have been the cause of much stunted growth. They have
weakened the feeling of *responsibility*, and diminished the
activity, of the Protestant communities; and, in addition, they
have aroused the not unfounded suspicion that the Church is an
institution set up by the State, and accordingly to be adjusted
to the State. Much has happened, indeed, in the last few decades

to check that suspicion by the greater independence which the Churches have obtained; but further progress in this direction is necessary, especially in regard to the freedom of individual communities. The connexion with the State must not be violently severed, for the Churches have derived much advantage from it; but steps must be taken to further the development upon which we have entered. If this results in multifarious organisations in the Church, it will do no harm; on the contrary, it will remind us, in a forcible way, that these forms are all arbitrary.

Further, Protestantism was forced by its opposition to Catholicism to lay exclusive emphasis on the inward character of religion, and upon "faith alone"; but to formulate one doctrine in sharp opposition to another is always a dangerous process. The man in the street is not sorry to hear that "good works" are unnecessary, nay, that they constitute a danger to the soul. Although Luther is not responsible for the convenient misunderstanding that ensued, the inevitable result was that in the reformed Churches in Germany from the very start there were accusations of moral laxity and a want of serious purpose in the sanctification of life. The saying "If ye love me, keep my commandments" was unwarrantably thrust into the background. Not until the Pietistic movement arose was its central importance once more recognised. Up till then the pendulum of the conduct of life took a suspicious swing in the contrary direction, out of opposition to the Catholic "justification by works." But religion is not only a state of the heart; it is a deed as well; it is faith active in love and in the sanctification of life. This is a truth with which Protestant Christians must become much better acquainted, if they are not to be put to shame.

There is another point closely connected with what I have just mentioned. The Reformation abolished monasticism, and was bound to abolish it. It rightly affirmed that to take a vow of lifelong asceticism was a piece of presumption; and it rightly considered that any worldly vocation, conscientiously followed in the sight of God, was equal to, nay, was better than, being a monk. But something now happened which Luther neither foresaw nor desired: "monasticism," of the kind that is conceivable and necessary in the Protestant sense of the word, disappeared altogether. Every community, however, stands in need of personalities living *exclusively* for its ends. The Church, for instance, needs volunteers who will abandon every other pursuit, renounce "the world," and devote themselves entirely to the service of their neighbour; not because such a vocation is "a higher one," but because it is a necessary one, and because no Church can live without also giving rise to this desire. But in the Protestant Churches the desire has been checked by the decided attitude which they have been compelled to adopt towards Catholicism. It is a high price that we have paid; nor can the price be reduced by considering, on the other hand, how much simple and unaffected religious fervour has been kindled in home and family life. We may rejoice, however, that in the past century a beginning has been made in the direction of re-couping this loss. In the institution of deaconesses and many cognate phenomena the Protestant Churches are getting back what they once rejected through their inability to recognise it in the form which it then took. But it must undergo a much ampler and more varied development.

Not only had the Reformation to pay a high price; it was also incapable of perceiving all the conclusions to which its new ideas led, and of giving them pure effect. It is not that the work which it did was not absolutely valid and permanent in every particular—how could that be, and who could desire it to have been so? No! it remained stationary in its development even at the point at which, to judge by the earnest foundation that was laid at the start, higher things might have been expected. Various causes combined to produce this result. From the year 1526 onwards national Churches had to be founded at headlong speed on Protestant lines; they were forced to be "rounded and complete" at a time when much was still in a state of flux. Then again, a mistrust of the left wing, of the "enthusiasts," induced the Churches to offer an energetic resistance to tendencies which they could have accompanied for a good bit of their way. Luther's unwillingness to have anything to do with them, nay, the manner in which he became suspicious of his own ideas when they coincided with those of the "enthusiasts," was bitterly avenged and came home to the Protestant Churches in the Age of Enlightenment. Even at the risk of being reckoned among Luther's detractors, we must go further. This genius had a faith as robust as Paul's, and thereby an immense power over the minds and hearts of men; but he was not abreast of the knowledge accessible even in his own time. The *naïve* age had gone by; it was an age of deep feeling, of progress, an age in which religion could not avoid contact with all the powers of mind. In this age it was his destiny to be forced to be not only a reformer but also *an intellectual and spiritual leader and teacher. The way of looking at the world and at history* he had to plan afresh for generations; for there was no one there to help him, and to no one else would people listen. But he had not all the resources of clear knowledge at his command. Lastly, he was always anxious to go back to the original, to the Gospel itself, and, so far as it was possible to do it by intuition and inward experience, he did it; moreover, he made some admirable studies in history, and in many places broke victoriously through the serried lines of the traditional dogmas. But any trustworthy knowledge of the history of those dogmas was as yet an impossibility, and still less was any historical acquaintance with the New Testament and primitive Christianity attainable. It is marvellous how in spite of all this Luther possessed so much power of penetration and sound judgment. We have only to look at his introductions to the books of the New Testament, or at his treatise on *Churches and Councils.* But there were countless problems of which he did not even know, to say nothing of being able to solve them; and so it was that he had no means of distinguishing between kernel and husk, between what was original and what was of alien growth. How can we be surprised then, if in its *doctrine*, and in *the view which it took of history*, the Reformation was far from being a finished product; and that, where it perceived no problems, confusion in its own ideas was inevitable? It could not, like Pallas Athene, spring complete from Jupiter's head; as doctrine it could do no more than mark a *beginning*, and it had to reckon on future development. But by being rapidly formed into national Churches it came near to itself cutting short its further development for all time.

As regards the confusion and the checks which it brought

upon itself, we must content ourselves with referring to a few leading points. Firstly, Luther would admit nothing but the Gospel, nothing but what frees and binds the consciences of men, what everyone, down to the man-servant and the maid-servant, can understand. But then he not only took the old dogmas of the Trinity and the two natures as part of the Gospel—he was not in a position to examine them historically—and even framed new ones, but he was absolutely incapable of making any sound distinction between "doctrine" and Gospel; in this respect falling far behind Paul. The necessary result was that intellectualism was still in the ascendant; that a scholastic doctrine was again set up as *necessary to salvation*; and that two classes of Christians once more arose : those who understand the doctrine, and the minors who are dependent on the others' understanding of it.

Secondly, Luther was convinced that that alone is the "Word of God" whereby a man is inwardly born anew—the message of the free grace of God in Christ. At the highest levels to which he attained in his life he was free from every sort of bondage to the letter. What a capacity he had for distinguishing between law and Gospel, between Old and New Testament, nay, for distinguishing in the New Testament itself! All that he would recognise was the kernel of the matter, clearly revealed as it is in these books, and proving its power by its effect on the soul. But he did not make a clean sweep. In cases where he had found the letter important, he demanded submission to the "it is written"; and he demanded it peremptorily, without recollecting that, where other sayings of the Scriptures were concerned, he himself had declared the "it is written" to be of no binding force.

Thirdly, grace is the forgiveness of sins, and therefore the assurance of possessing a God of grace, and life, and salvation. How often Luther repeated this, always with the addition that what was efficacious here was the *Word*—that union of the soul with God in the trust and childlike reverence which God's Word inspires; it was a *personal* relation which was here involved. But the same man allowed himself to be inveigled into the most painful controversies about the means of grace, about communion and infant baptism. These were struggles in which he ran the

risk of again exchanging his high conception of grace for the
Catholic conception, as well as of sacrificing the fundamental
idea that it is a purely spiritual possession that is in question,
and that, compared with Word and faith, all else is of no importance. What he here bequeathed to his Church has become a
legacy of woe.

Fourthly, the counter-Church which, as was inevitable, rapidly
arose in opposition to the Roman Church, and under the pressure
which that Church exercised, perceived, not without reason, that
its truth and its title lay in the re-establishment of the Gospel.
But whilst the counter-Church privily identified the sum and
substance of its doctrine with the Gospel, the thought also stole
in surreptitiously: *We*, that is to say, the particular Churches
which had now sprung up, *are the true Church*. Luther, of
course, was never able to forget that the true Church was the
sacred community of the faithful; but still he had no clear ideas
as to the relation between it and the visible new Church which
had now arisen, and subsequent generations settled down more
and more into the sad misunderstanding: We are the true
Church *because we have the right "doctrine."* This misunderstanding, besides giving rise to evil results in self-infatuation and
intolerance, still further strengthened that mischievous distinction between theologians and clergy on the one side, and the
laity on the other, on which we have already dwelt. Not, perhaps,
in theory, but certainly in practice, a double form of Christianity
arose, just as in Catholicism; and in spite of the efforts of the
Pietistic movement it still remains with us to-day. The theologian
and the clergyman must defend *the whole doctrine* and be
orthodox; for the layman it suffices if he adheres to certain
leading points and refrains from attacking the orthodox creed.
A very well-known man, as I have been lately told, expressed
the wish that a certain inconvenient theologian would go over
to the philosophical faculty; "for then," he said, "instead of an
unbelieving theologian we should have a believing philosopher."
Here we have the logical outcome of the contention that in the
Protestant Churches, too, doctrine is something laid down for all
time, and that in spite of being generally binding it is a matter
of so much difficulty that the laity need not be expected to defend

it. But if we persist on this path, and other confusions become worse confounded and take firmer root, there is a risk of Protestantism becoming a sorry double of Catholicism. I say a sorry double, because there are two things which Protestantism will never obtain, namely, a pope and monastic priests. Neither the letter of the Bible nor any belief embodied in creeds can ever produce the unconditional authority which Catholics possess in the Pope; and Protestantism cannot now return to the monastic priest. It retains its national Churches and its married clergy, neither of which looks very stately by the side of Catholicism, if competition with Catholicism is what the Protestant Churches desire.

Gentlemen, Protestantism is not yet, thank God, in such a bad way that the imperfections and confusions in which it began have got the upper hand and entirely stunted or stifled its true character. Even those among us who are convinced that the Reformation in the sixteenth century is something that is over and done with, are by no means ready to abandon the momentous ideas on which it was based, and there is a large field in which all earnest Protestant Christians are in complete unanimity. But if those who think that the Reformation is done with cannot see that its continuance in the sense of a pure understanding of God's Word is a question of life and death for Protestantism— its continuance has already borne abundant fruit in associations like the *Evangelical Union*—let them at least promote the liberty for which Luther fought in his best days : "Let the minds of men rush one against another and strike; if some are meanwhile led astray—well! that is what we must expect in war; where there is battle and slaughter, some must fall and be wounded, but whoso fights honestly will receive the crown."

The reason why the catholicising of the Protestant Churches —I do not mean that they are becoming papal; I mean that they are becoming Churches of ordinance, doctrine, and ceremony—is so burning a question is that three powerful forces are working together to further this development. First, there is the indifference of the masses. The tendency of all indifference is to put religion on the same plane with authority and tradition, but also with priests, hierarchies, and the cult of ceremonies. It

puts religion there, and then goes on to complain of the external
character and stationary condition of religion, and of the "pretensions" of the clergy; nay, it is capable apparently, at one
and the same moment, of mingling those complaints with abuse,
of contemptuously jeering at every active expression of religious
feeling, and doing homage to every kind of ceremony. This kind
of indifference has no understanding whatever for Protestant
Christianity, instinctively tries to suppress it, and praises
Catholicism at its expense. The second of the forces to be taken
into consideration is what I may call "the natural religion"—
I mean the religion of those who live by fear and hope; whose
chief endeavour is to find some authority in matters of religion;
who are eager to be rid of their own responsibility and want to
be reassured; who are looking for some "adjunct" to life, whether
in its solemn hours or in its worst distress, some æsthetic transfiguration, or some violent form of assistance till time itself assists.
All these people are also, without being aware of it, putting
religion on the Catholic plane; they want "something that they
can lean upon," and a good deal else, too—all kinds of things
to stir them up and help them; but they do not want the
Christianity of the Gospel. But the Christianity of the Gospel
in yielding to such demands becomes Catholic Christianity. The
third force I mention unwillingly, and yet I cannot pass it over
in silence; it is the *State*. We must not blame the State for setting
chief store by the conservative influence which religion and the
Churches exercise, and the subsidiary effects which they produce
in respect of reverence, obedience, and public order. But this is
just the reason why the State exercises pressure in this direction,
protects all the elements of stability in the Churches, and seeks to
keep them from every inner movement that would call their
unity and their "public utility" in question; nay, it has tried
often enough to approximate the Church to the police, and
employ it as a means of maintaining order in the State. We can
pardon this—let the State take the means of power wherever
it can find them; but the Church must not allow itself to be made
into a pliant instrument; for, side by side with all the desolating
consequences to its vocation and prestige, it would thereby
become an outward institution in which public order is of greater

consequence than the spirit, form more important than matter, and obedience of higher value than truth.

In the face of these three so different forces, what we have to do is to maintain Christian earnestness and liberty as presented in the Gospel. Theology alone is unavailing; what is wanted is firmness of Christian character. The Protestant Churches will be pushed into the background if they do not make a stand. It was out of such free creations as the Pauline communities were that the Catholic Church once arose. Who can guarantee that those Churches, too, will not become "Catholic" which had their origin in "the liberty of a Christian man"?

That, however, would not involve the destruction of the Gospel : so much, at least, history proves. It would be still traceable like a red thread in the centre of the web, and somewhere or other it would emerge afresh, and free itself from its entangling connexions. Even in the outwardly decorated but inwardly decayed temples of the Greek and Roman Church it has not been effaced. "Venture onwards! deep down in a vault you will still find the altar and its sacred, ever-burning lamp!" This Gospel, associated as it was with the speculative ideas and the mystery-worship of the Greeks, yet did not perish in them; united with the Roman empire, it held its own even in this fusion, nay, out of it gave birth to the Reformation. Its dogmatic doctrines, its ordinances of public worship, have changed; nay, what is much more, it has been embraced by the simplest and purest minds and by the greatest thinkers; it endeared itself to a St. Francis and to a Newton. It has outlived all the changing philosophies of the world; it has cast off like a garment forms and ideas which were once sacred; it has participated in the entire progress of civilisation; it has become spiritualised, and in the course of history it has learnt how to make a surer application of its ethical principles. In its original earnestness and in the consolation which it offers, it has come home to thousands in all ages; and in all ages, too, it has thrown off all its encumbrances, and broken down all barriers. If we were right in saying that the Gospel is the knowledge and recognition of God as the Father, the certainty of redemption, humility and joy in God, energy and brotherly love; if it is essential to this religion that the founder must not be forgotten over his message, nor the message over the founder, history shows us that the Gospel has, in point of fact, remained in force, struggling again and again to the surface.

You will perhaps have felt that I have not entered into present questions, the relation, namely, of the Gospel to our present intellectual condition, our whole knowledge of the world, and our task therein. But to do this with any success in regard to the actual situation of affairs would require longer than a few fleeting hours. As regards the kernel of the matter, however, I have said all that is needful, *for no new phase in the history of the Christian Religion has occurred since the Reformation.* Our knowledge of the world has undergone enormous changes— every century since the Reformation marks an advance, the most important being those in the last two; but, looked at from a religious and ethical point of view, the forces and principles of the Reformation have not been outrun or rendered obsolete. We need only grasp them in their purity and courageously apply them, and modern ideas will not put any *new* difficulties in their way. *The real difficulties in the way of the religion of the Gospel remain the old ones.* In face of them we can "prove" nothing, for our proofs are only variations of our convictions. But the course which history has taken has surely opened up a wide province, in which the Christian sense of brotherhood must give practical proof of itself quite otherwise than it knew how, or was able, to do in the early centuries—I mean the social province. Here a tremendous task confronts us, and in the measure in which we accomplish it shall we be able to answer with a better heart the deepest of all questions—*the question of the meaning of life.*

Gentlemen, it is religion, the love of God and neighbour, which gives life a meaning; knowledge cannot do it. Let me, if you please, speak of my own experience, as one who for thirty years has taken an earnest interest in these things. Pure knowledge is a glorious thing, and woe to the man who holds it light or blunts his sense for it. But to the question, Whence, whither, and to what purpose, it gives an answer to-day as little as it did two or three thousand years ago. It does, indeed, instruct us in facts; it detects inconsistencies; it links phenomena; it corrects the deceptions of sense and idea. But where and how the curve of the world and the curve of our own life begin—that curve of which it shows us only a section—and whither this curve leads, knowledge does not tell us. Yet if with a steady will we affirm the forces and the standards which on the summits of our inner life shine out as our highest good, nay, as our real self; if we are earnest and courageous enough to accept them as the great Reality and direct our lives by them; and if we then look at the course of mankind's history, follow its upward development, and search, in strenuous and patient service, for the communion of minds in it, we shall not faint in weariness and despair, but become certain of God, of the God whom Jesus Christ called his Father, and who is also our Father.

Made and printed in Great Britain by
The Garden City Press Limited
Letchworth · Hertfordshire